Between Each Step is t
wants to read when th
them. Equal parts trail beta, local color, and natural history laced with personality and passion for life as a professional vagabond, Patrice has brought New Zealand's epic Te Araroa to life. One thing's for sure, this trail is now on my bucket list.

> ~ *Kristin Hostetter, Editor-in-Chief of SNEWS and The Voice, and former Gear Editor at Backpacker*

Patrice's vivid stories took me back to my travels through New Zealand with my husband. Her detailed account of her Te Araroa journey with Justin reminds me of how beautifully imperfect relationships can be—and how transformative Mother Nature is for everyone.

> ~ *Heather Balogh Rochfort, writer and author*

This is truly a memoir for the road less travelled—not simply because Te Araroa is just now becoming a more sought-after adventure for thru hikers, but because Patrice and Justin La Vigne laid aside societal expectations and followed their hearts (and feet!). In their journey, you'll find inspiration to collect experiences, steeped in nature, adventure, and joy. Oh, and you'll get some great and very real insights into trail life too!

> ~ *D. Luke Iorio, PCC, podcaster, coach, and wide-angled observer, former CEO and President of the Institute for Professional Excellence in Coaching (iPEC)*

BETWEEN
EACH
STEP

A MARRIED COUPLE'S THRU HIKE
ON NEW ZEALAND'S TE ARAROA

By Patrice La Vigne

atmosphere press

Copyright © 2020 Between Each Step

Cover design by Nick Courtright
Cover images provided by the author

Published by Atmosphere Press

No part of this book may be reproduced
except in brief quotations and in reviews
without permission from the publisher.

Between Each Step
2020, Patrice La Vigne

atmospherepress.com

For Justin, my lifelong adventure partner—
and honestly—my secret to success.

| Foreword |

By Mark Weatherall,
Chief Executive of Te Araroa Trust
– New Zealand's Trail

It was an honor to be asked to write the foreword for this book because this story and its author embody how to enjoy Te Araroa responsibly and fully. Patrice and her husband had one heck of an adventure on the trail. Te Araroa is a very unique track, and I believe Patrice has caught the essence of New Zealand's natural environment, culture, history and people in her book. With her Leave No Trace and backpacking experience, she sets a good example and influence for future walkers.

Since its opening in 2011 and since Patrice hiked in 2014-15, Te Araroa has changed quite a bit. For one, there are a lot more people doing the track now! In the summer of 2019, we had 1500 thru walkers and tens of thousands of section walkers. In comparison, only thirty people attempted a thru hike in 2011 when it opened.

Patrice and Justin were fortunate in some ways to experience the trail in its early days because of the lack of trampers. But, of course, with that, they had to overcome many challenges that we don't have these days. It's fair to say that our mapping and trail notes are better now! We even have an app for that!

I have been the chief executive of Te Araroa Trust since 2018. I have lived in New Zealand all my life and come from a very outdoor-oriented family. I studied parks and recreation at university, and after twenty years in sports management, becoming the chief executive was an opportunity to get back into the outdoors.

The trail has the same challenges any trail does with growing pains, rerouting sections and relationships with private landowners. There have been issues with litter and other waste as the popularity increases. And while the majority of walkers are respectful, it's important to have ongoing education for all trail users.

I highly recommend this book, as you won't be disappointed. You'll be masterfully guided through New Zealand. And because of Patrice's special style of writing, once you start reading, it's really hard to put the book down!

| Contents |

| 1 |

Not Your Normal Beach
Days 1-4: 62.8 miles

Our trail notes do not recommend crossing the short, rocky section in high tide. We've only hiked a single mile on our first day on New Zealand's Te Araroa and already we encounter an obstacle.

It is 1:30 P.M. and low tide isn't until 5 P.M. We have two choices: cross the dissuaded rocky section at high tide or find another route using the boulder skyscraper above us.

I see peaceful green pastures towering three hundred feet overhead. I squint into the sun, following a faint line that could be a trail beyond the cliffs, offering a safe alternative.

"I read on someone's blog that it's an extra four miles to hike around those cliffs," I bellow over the roaring sea to my husband and hiking partner, Justin.

"Ugh," is his response. "Is there no other way around this?"

We observe the ocean patterns for a few minutes from the safety of the beach. The wind is powering the surf so that the waves obscure the typical path and crash about a foot up the cliff wall. A patch of dry, safe sand stretches beyond the saltwater course.

"Can you see?" Justin points toward our ocean path. "It's only a five-foot section that will be tricky."

When the current ebbs, we have a full thirty seconds to scramble across the craggy rocks that stick out like teeth.

Pigeon-sized butterflies gather in my stomach. "I don't know," I choke. "This makes me nervous."

Justin is still watching the ocean contemplatively. I step off into the grassy area, trying to get a better look up at Plan B. Either the trail is extremely overgrown, or I am just not focusing on the right spot, because I detect nothing reassuring.

"I think we can do this," Justin urges.

"We should wait another hour at least," I appeal, biting the inside of my cheek.

"I don't want to wait. I don't want to add extra miles onto our first day," Justin whines. "I'll go first and make sure it's doable." I fill my lungs with a deep breath and exhale slowly, attempting to control my rapid heart rate.

"As soon as the waves crash, that's our moment to get moving," Justin continues casually. "Don't stop, don't look back, and just remember what you know about rock climbing. If a swell hits you, just hold on, wait a moment for it to recede, then continue." He takes one more hard look at the ocean and looks back at me. I wonder if that's a grimace I see on his face, and if there's dread building underneath his sunglasses. He shouts, "Ready?" I nod my head with false bravado, gritting my teeth all the while.

My eyes follow as Justin glides across the rock face effortlessly. Less than twenty seconds later, he gives me the thumbs up from the other side.

His smooth crossing gives me the silent courage I am yearning for. I scrutinize the whitecaps as they reach the crag. I say a short prayer that a rogue wave doesn't overtake me on the first day of our grand adventure.

I quicken my movements when the crest recedes and focus my eyes on the black, wet rock face I am nearly kissing. My fingers claw and clench anything I can find. The shelf handholds feel strong, but my legs shake as my feet skate across the greasy slabs. I taste the salt in the air. Justin reaches his hand out to guide me on the last two steps. I hear the wave break just as I am landing my last foot on stable ground.

Seven miles later, we reach our first camp spot of the trip, Twilight Beach. While gazing out to the sparkling aquamarine Tasman Sea, I open my backpack and pull out our 2014 Thanksgiving feast in the form of a dehydrated meal—chicken and noodles.

I quirk my mouth in a small smile, remembering how just four days earlier, we were sweating bullets on the Auckland airport line wondering if our meals would make it through New Zealand customs.

Back in America, a few months ago, we purchased seventy-six Backpackers Pantry dehydrated meals for our planned thru hike of Te Araroa, the newest long-distance, continuous hike in the world that stretches three thousand kilometers (more than two thousand miles) from the top of New Zealand at Cape Reinga southbound to the bottom at Bluff. The meals were our biggest concern coming into the country. New Zealand has very strict biosecurity regulations—heck, you had to make sure there was not a speck of dirt on your hiking boots. So when we scoured other hikers' blogs and read multiple accounts of food confiscations, we became worried. The Ministry for Primary Industries website listed allowances for non-liquid food, moisture-reduced food and other categories. But, after scrolling through the bureaucratic site, I came away with more questions than answers. Toting seventy-six meals through customs was certainly going to be a stretch given the guidelines, but we took our chances. We are admittedly lazy backpackers, so we want to do nothing more than boil two cups of water for dinner, and we needed these meals to keep up our low-fuss camper dinner routine. They are cheaper in the United States, so the risk was worthwhile.

On November 26, 2014, we stood in Auckland airport's customs line at 6 A.M. with our passenger cards claiming food and camping equipment.

"Next!" the bald agent in a light blue button-down shirt waved us over and reached out to grab our passenger cards. "You got fruit?"

"No," Justin said. I let him do the talking. This was the moment of truth, and I felt like I was going to vomit or have a royal case of the runs.

The agent spilled the meals from our packs. I felt silly seeing them strewn about on the metal table. He picked up three of them and took them over to the computer. Justin tried to make conversation, offering some information about the meals, but the man continued to concentrate on the task at hand. Eyes hollowed under tired brows, he read package label after package label, typing ingredients into the computer.

He carried the meals back over to the table.

"You're good to go," he said with a toothy grin. The carefreeness in his Kiwi accent could not be mistaken. "But, you know we hev food in New Zealand, ay?"

We finish our Thanksgiving feast on Twilight Beach and though it is only 6 P.M., we both decide to lie down in the tent.

"Just going to rest my eyes for a few minutes," Justin whispers. Drunk with euphoria from our first day on the trail, I agree and let my shoulders sink into my Therm-a-Rest sleeping pad, closing my eyes and basking in the sun's warmth still soaring over the sea. The splish-splash of waves lulls me to sleep.

Four hours later, we wake to find our sleeping bags soaked with dew.

"I forgot about the sea air," Justin laughs, looking around his now opaline bed. The last lances of light are casting down as the night sky sets in. We emerge to put the rainfly on our tent. By the end of our trek, we'd be able to count on one hand how many times we could sleep without our rainfly. No matter where you are in New Zealand, you are never more than seventy-nine miles from the sea.

The first sixty plus miles, or one hundred kilometers, of Te Araroa follows Ninety Mile Beach. I remember reading previous hikers' blogs complaining about the beach walking, and thinking they were wimps. Who doesn't love beach walking?

By mid-morning on day two, my feet are throbbing. I don't love beach walking. When I think of beaches, I think of coolers full of beer and sodas, sun bathing and building sandcastles. There is sand and sun on New Zealand's Ninety Mile Beach, but people? No way. This beach is as rugged as it gets. The goal for the first four days of Te Araroa is to keep the dunes on the left and the sea on the right. Simple as that. Eventually, the rhythm of the heaving wave music becomes no more than a murmur.

In the afternoon, I struggle to get my mind to hitch a ride to a happy place, but my focus is on the discomfort radiating from my tender feet. Knowing I am prone to blisters, especially during multi-day backpacking trips, I tried everything I could in preparation for this long hike. I even tried to toughen my skin by soaking my feet in tincture of benzoin the week before we left. But of course, I still develop blisters.

I long to take a break, but this deserted beach lacks shelter. I gasp as I see a small piece of driftwood up ahead. Objects on the beach always appear a lot closer than they are, but I'm fairly certain this is in our very near future.

I motion to the chunk of timber and yell to Justin in the most affirmative tone I can, "Break!"

He pulls out his ear bud. "You want a break up there?"

Without slowing my march or looking at him, I blurt, "Yes." That's what I already said, I think in my head.

As soon as I see the driftwood, I jog, unfastening my backpack hip belt and chest strap in the process. The wood is smaller than it looked. There is only room for one person.

"I'll stand," Justin says.

"Thank you."

I take my shoe and sock off from my right foot and immediately start massaging it.

"Your feet hurt?"

"Yes. They're throbbing."

"God. It's only day two," he snorts. "Did you try to adjust your socks? Or loosen your laces?" He's always trying to fix things.

"I'll be fine. I just need a minute to get the blood flowing." I take my shoe and sock off from my left foot and wonder how I'm going to make it the subsequent twenty-five miles of the beach.

Minutes later, I reluctantly retie my boots and let the lifeless thirty-five-pound backpack become an extension of my shoulders and reshape my torso again.

What seems like an eternity later, we bed down for the night at a section on the map marked The Bluff, behind the dunes, where the grass on the knoll is dancing in the wind and almost waving us over. Justin shoulders the load of camp duties so I can tend to my feet.

We sit on the dune hill eating our Beef Stroganoff dehydrated meal and watching the tumultuous Tasman Sea swallow the ember red sun.

"I can't believe we're in New Zealand. I love it here," I beam. "Isn't this gorgeous?" Justin gives my hand a squeeze in agreement. Justin is the more immunocompromised one out of the two of us, so sometimes I don't think he knows how to react when I am the one with a problem. Thankfully, happy feet turn me back into my happy self.

"How are you feeling?" I ask. "Is your stomach or your legs bothering you?"

Justin has had Crohn's disease since he was a teenager. It's a chronic inflammatory bowel disease that affects his gastrointestinal tract, and has other far-reaching complications. When I met Justin in 2002, he was in remission. He wasn't on any maintenance medication, but stayed active and knew what foods he had to avoid, such as nuts, seeds and raw vegetables, to keep the disease at bay. I remember his mom saying to me before we got married, "I hope Justin has a flare up that puts him in the hospital before you get married." The statement struck me as odd, but she really wanted me to understand the kind of patient Justin was and hardships Crohn's could bring. He had occasional flare-ups over the years with increased stomach pain and joint pain, but for the most part, Crohn's did not impact our life yet.

"I'm okay. Just tired. I think I'm gonna lie down in the tent."

"Just going to rest your eyes?" I tease.

"Only for a little bit!" he defends. "You coming?"

"No, I think I'll stay here for a little bit."

The waves of the Tasman Sea mesmerize me. The Tasman Sea. Who ever thought I'd be gazing out onto it?

Justin and I always wanted to go to New Zealand. When we got engaged in 2005, we talked about going for our honeymoon. But it was completely unrealistic. We were paying for bits and pieces of our wedding, had just bought a house built in the 1880s that had multiple holes in the roof and needed a slew of renovations and we had a combined savings of $10,000. New Zealand was an expensive country to visit, so it would have been a very irresponsible adult decision.

The subject of New Zealand came up again in 2011 while we were thru hiking the Appalachian Trail. We had built our savings enough to be able to leave our jobs to go hiking. We chose the atypical southbound route on the Appalachian Trail for our first thru hike.

Going southbound meant we met the hordes of thru hikers heading northbound nearly every day in Maine, New Hampshire, Vermont and Massachusetts. It was July 8, 2011, and we were camped at Eliza Brook Shelter in New Hampshire, which was packed with seven Appalachian Trail northbounders. One girl was from New Zealand, so naturally we picked her brain. She described Te Araroa. Translating to "The Long Pathway" in Maori, this trail, stretching the length of New Zealand across both islands, was set to open December 3, 2011. We needed no convincing, merely on the idea that there is no better way to explore our dream country than via foot, in our minds.

Seed planted, I did my research in the years following our Appalachian Trail thru hike. I read *Te Araroa: The New Zealand Trail - One Man Walks His Dream*, written by Geoff Chapple, creator of the trail. In 1998, Geoff walked the proposed trail, long before it was ready for the public. He worked tirelessly through the years to make the long pathway a reality. I appreciated his vision and tenacity.

I devoured blogs of other walkers, though there were very few, given the trail's infancy. I found out two of our Appalachian Trail friends, Clara and BJ, had done it in 2013. Week after week, I would send Clara a myriad of questions to help in my planning.

Though the Appalachian Trail and Te Araroa are both roughly eighteen inches wide by two thousand miles—the Appalachian Trail being 2,181 miles the year we hiked—the two trails couldn't differ more if they were an orange and a carrot. Perhaps the biggest factor was that Te Araroa measured everything in kilometers, rather than miles, and meters, rather than feet. Math was not my thing, but I am slowly learning how to convert. Beyond math, this trail had challenges you would never see on American long-distance trails, like the tides we encountered on our first day.

Still, the allure of New Zealand and walking another long-distance trail was prevalent for us. In the summer of 2014, we decided we had saved enough money to disappear into the wilderness again. And as a fall breeze swept through the air in the Northern Hemisphere, we clicked "purchase" on tickets that would fly us into a second summer in the Southern Hemisphere. We would treat the hike as more of a vacation than just a hike, splurging on side trips for sightseeing and regular town visits to enjoy food and lodging.

My reminiscing is broken by what appears to be a figure walking on the beach. Clara and BJ had advised us to bring a monocular on this hike, but we failed to listen. I raise my sunglasses and focus my eyes to assess the situation better. I am certain it is not a hallucination, but a person, and not just any person—a backpacker.

I run over to our tent. "There's another hiker! There's another hiker!"

I sprint back over to the dune, watching as the hiker—who I now realize is a female—nears closer and closer. It's only been two days since we've seen anyone, but it feels like an eternity. Seeing another hiker out here would assure me we are not the only crazy ones. I try hard to contain my excitement as I yell out, "Hey!" She continues her steps, so I turn up the decibels. "Hey!"

She pulls ear buds out and walks in my direction.

"Are you hiking Te Araroa?" she asks, stopping to catch her breath.

"Yes!" I respond. "My husband and I are."

"Are you camping here tonight?"

"Yes. Right over there behind the dune," I point.

"Is it windy? I tried to set up my tent in two other spots, but the wind was too much and I couldn't stake it down."

"No, our spot is sheltered," I say in a persuasive tone.

"Do you mind if I camp here with you guys?"

"Not at all!"

We learn that Marilyne is a thirty-something hiker from Montreal. She started at Cape Reinga today, meaning she hiked nearly twenty-five miles on her first day. She apologizes after a short conversation, saying she is beat and going to retire to her tent without dinner. I don't blame her. I'm ready for bed after my seventeen miles of walking.

We pack up camp the next morning before Marilyne and wish her well, certain we will see her later that day.

Day three's miles pass slowly. While the ocean soundtrack is beautiful, donning our own music helps ease the monotony that beach walking has created. Ocean, sand, shells, seaweed, dead fish, repeat. There is a serious lack of diversity on the beaches. I now know how I will meet my demise: death by boredom. On the drive up to Te Araroa's starting point at Cape Reinga's iconic lighthouse, our tour bus driver told us a torpedo once washed up on Ninety Mile Beach. Now that would make things interesting.

I look behind me and can barely make out a figure, presumably Marilyne. I turn and continue to follow Justin's footprints, tiny divots in the vast sand. Goddamn beach. It's more like concrete. Goddamn feet. I want so much to enjoy myself, but all I can think about is the soreness. I feel like a collapsing umbrella, battling the winds on a stormy day.

"Punching in a Dream" by the Naked and Famous queues up on my playlist.

Way-yay-yay-yay-yay, I don't ever wanna be here. / Like punching in a dream breathing life into my nightmare. / If it falls apart, I would surely wake it. / Bright lights turn me clean, this is worse than it seems.

Oh my God. Is my dream vacation turning into my nightmare? From the blister forming under my toenail to the piercing agony I feel in my hips, I wonder if I am writing checks my body can't cash.

I didn't start my love of the outdoors until my early twenties. My family was not into the outdoors. My father fought in the Vietnam War and he'd sworn off nature, thanks to his thirteen months spent in the jungle trenches.

"I want to spend the rest of my life indoors after experiencing 115 degrees living like a pig in the mud surrounded by twelve-foot snakes and twelve-inch centipedes," my dad would repeat over and over again.

My mother, on the other hand, loved beaches. Growing up, my sister and I would spend our summer days hatless and lathered in Coppertone Sun Tan Lotion SPF 4 swimming in lakes.

But hiking, climbing mountains, paddling and backpacking? I had to discover the love all on my own. As an adolescent, I used to climb as high as I could in the trees, explore my backyard woods until poison ivy covered me from head to toe and fight with my mom about wasting my time taking a bath. It was inevitable I would be an outdoor gal.

Fresh out of college, I moved from the East Coast to

Phoenix, Arizona. I was participating in a year-long post-college volunteer program. I shared a house with five other males and females. We all worked full-time jobs, but instead of receiving our full paychecks, the money was filtered into the volunteer program and we each received a $65 per month stipend. Our housing and food was budgeted from a communal fund, but the $65 per month was ours to do what we pleased.

Living in a big city with $65 per month as my spending money limited my options. Phoenix is a city, but unlike the cities I knew from the East Coast, it is surrounded by undeveloped land and trails for hiking. I met a group of ladies who hiked up a local mountain every morning at 5 A.M. before work. Needing some sort of no-cost hobby, I thought I should join them. It became my routine, my outlet, my sanity. I was already a runner who experienced life in a slower pace than a car, but hiking brought me to wild spaces and really made me appreciate the details of my surroundings.

I met Justin in Phoenix a few months later at an adult hiking club. He was getting his master's in Recreation Management and Tourism, a major I didn't even know existed. He told me on our first date his goal was to walk the Appalachian Trail.

"The Appalachian Trail? That's cool. What's that?" I asked innocently.

Apparently, I grew up in New Jersey forty minutes from the Delaware Water Gap trailhead on the Appalachian Trail, but had no idea.

After dating my tried-and-true mountain man for just a few weeks, I was wooed enough by his wild-minded spirit and promise of unknown—but unforgettable—paths to know he was my soul mate. I was still a newbie hiker, but through his knowledge and experience I evolved into a more confident, dedicated and flexible backpacker. The allure of hiking became ingrained within me as if it was something I'd loved since in utero.

Reminding myself that this is my dream vacation and I am a backpacker, I forge forward, white-knuckling my trekking poles. The headwind on the beach is relentless and I bite back tears.

I am an adventurer. I love backpacking. I repeat these statements to myself and slowly, they put me back on track.

I see Justin way up ahead, walking confidently, and I speed up to catch up.

I am an adventurer. I love backpacking.

When Justin sees me at his side, he stops and plays air guitar with his trekking pole, bouncing his head to a drum rhythm.

He pulls his ear bud out, "Can you guess what song that is?"

"Um," I stop and ponder. Justin loves music, so it could be anything from bluegrass to classic rock.

"It's Bon Jovi's *Livin' On A Prayer*!" he exclaims. "Perfect cause we're more than halfway done with the beach!"

My husband knows me too well. That silly pick-me-up is all I need to keep going.

By the end of the day, we start seeing more traffic on the shoreline—five tour buses, fourteen cars and seven motorized bikes. I still fantasize about being seated on the Sand Safaris tour bus that dropped us at Cape Reinga days ago. But I also remind myself to embrace the moment, as my memories of beach walking will be bittersweet soon enough.

Marilyne never does catch up. We call it a day after twenty-two miles of walking. I sleep well that night in the dunes, knowing tomorrow we will reach the village of Ahipara, the end of the beach.

We wake to more wind, but I am grateful for the breeze to balance out the sun frying its way through our sunscreen. If the sun is this hot during New Zealand's spring, I wonder what summer will be like in a few weeks. The ozone layer is thinner in New Zealand, plus there is very little air pollution, both of which create a terrible recipe for skin cancer.

By 11 A.M. on day four, we say goodbye to the beach. There are a lot of people around the entrance of Ahipara. They give us funny looks. We head out further to the road for a better chance at sticking our thumbs out to snag a ride to resupply in Kaitaia. We wave to the police vehicle towing a car from the sand.

Justin boldly states, "I'm going to ask that police officer about where the best place is to hitch to Kaitaia." Justin is never afraid to ask anyone for anything, whereas I choose the path of least resistance if it means bothering people less.

I stand back, slightly embarrassed, but I overhear the uniformed man respond with, "Why would you wont to hitchhike? I'll just give you a lift!"

This would never happen in America, I think.

"One of you can hop in the front," he encourages.

I accidentally open the driver's side door to get in.

"Oops," I stammer. "We're from the States."

Even though I desperately want to shed my boots, I

resist the urge, sparing the policeman a horrific, lingering stench in his vehicle.

Twenty minutes later, we pull up to Main Street Lodge in Kaitaia. I let Justin grab the packs and I sit to peel off my boots and socks before going into the hostel office. Everyone seems to walk around barefooted in New Zealand, so I assure myself I haven't quite lost all my dignity.

Barefooted hostel manager, Henrick, checks us in, giving us the same private room we had when we started here four days ago. Kaitaia is the closest full-service town to the trail's starting point at Cape Reinga. Tour buses often shuttle sightseers up to the promontory for a view of the Pacific Ocean meeting the Tasman Sea, blending two colors and two tides. Killing two birds with one stone, the tour companies add hikers to their load for a small one-way fee. Otherwise, hikers try their hand at hitching the few hours to the out-of-the way vacation attraction.

Henrick looks down at my desquamated, blistering feet and says, "Ouch."

"What? These?" I say, while gingerly shifting my weight from one foot to the other and desperately trying not to flinch. "Totally normal."

As we settle in, Justin asks if he should just walk the mile to the grocery store by himself, citing my destroyed feet. I could hug him, if I had any energy. We typically do all the shopping together, even in regular life. I am the compulsive list maker who shops according to planned out meals, mainly for budgeting reasons, but also because I know myself, and trying to whip something up from whatever ingredients we have on hand would just stress me out unnecessarily. I force Justin to come grocery shopping because he is fussier than I am, mainly due to his gut issues and fluctuating appetite. His dietary sensitivities do not fit into a specific category and can change on a dime.

I know Justin can handle this grocery store visit solo though. We only need a few lunch items, as we left a bag of rations full of our dehydrated meals, snacks we brought from America and oatmeal packets stashed at the hostel for this ensuing leg.

Resupplying in New Zealand is a little different than it would be in America. For our Appalachian Trail thru hike, I had a chart with two columns. One listed twelve places without services to mail ourselves packages full of meals and snacks. The other listed twenty-five towns with grocery stores—as detailed as listing the store name— where we could buy our provisions on the spot. All of that information was readily available.

For New Zealand, I knew of five places on the South Island where resupply options were limited, and we could mail packages full of our dehydrated dinners and other favorites from the States. Otherwise, the nature of the trail and country stumped my knowledge and ability to form a plan of action for resupplying. From Te Araroa alumni, I knew we would pass towns on the North Island every one-to-six days. What we could find in the stores was totally unpredictable. Trail food is not an exact science; I had to throw caution to the wind. This was one of the many ways Te Araroa would teach me to fill my life with a little more Zen.

My feet burn in the shower, but I know it is good to clean the hot spots and let them air out. Upon closer examination, it is clear I would lose one toenail, maybe two. My feet are delicate and I never fail to acquire a few blisters during the first few days of hiking.

There is a constant debate in hiker circles about whether high-top hiking boots versus lightweight trail runners are better. I've always been a boot girl, while Justin has been a trail runner guy. For Te Araroa, I convinced him heartier shoes were necessary, as Kiwi trails have a reputation for being rugged. Boots may not have been adequate for the three-day beach walk, but I am confident he will thank me later when he sees the upcoming terrain.

I keep both feet elevated as I bring up the painstakingly slow Internet to work on my first blog post of our trek. There are virtual high fives and 'hell yeahs' across the Pacific waiting in our e-mail inbox. It makes me smile.

Justin returns a little over an hour later with peanut butter, jelly and sandwich thins for our trail lunches.

"They don't carry tuna in packets, only cans," he apologizes. "And this store didn't have any salami and cheese. I know the peanut butter and jelly is heavy, but our options were limited."

"No, you've done well!" I assure him, still thankful I didn't have to walk to the grocery store.

We cook up some dinner before retiring to bed by 9 P.M. Unfortunately, the other hostel guests have alternate plans in the common area near our room and keep us up until 1 A.M., despite Justin asking them to quiet down three times. Such is hostel life.

The next morning, we call our two-year-old nephew on Justin's side to wish him a Happy Birthday before we leave the hostel. Though it is December 1 for us in New Zealand, it is still November 30 in the United States.

Justin's family in Denver, Colorado, is eighteen hours behind us, while my family on the East Coast is sixteen hours behind us.

Justin and I roam the streets trying to find the best place to hitchhike. We made a sign saying "Ahipara", but Justin is holding it against his side as we walk down the road toward the corner.

A woman in a white car pulls over.

"Is she pulling over for us?" I ask.

"Doubt it."

But as we get closer to her parked car, she hoots out the window, "I had a hard time reading your sign because it was turned down, but hop in! I can take you to Ahipara!"

She is happy to have company on her drive to work in Ahipara. She has five kids and has never heard of Te Araroa. This will become a trend among most of the Kiwis we meet. New Zealand is full of hitchhikers, but not as dirty and smelly as we are. With people not knowing much about the trail, it must terrify them to see us.

We road walk to the start of the infamous four forests, which will take us across the middle of the Northland from the Tasman Sea to the Pacific Ocean. For those who survive the beach, many meet their demise in the bush.

| 2 |

Mudtastic Jungles
Days 5-9: 73.2 miles

The first thing I notice in the Herekino Forest is not the mud, but the birdsong. After hearing the sound of constant crashing waves the past few days, I smile.

Is it a bellbird? A fantail? A mockingjay? Oh wait, mockingjays are the fictitious birds from *The Hunger Games*.

I later find out it is a tui. The tui's chorus is not a traditional "cheep cheep," nor is it a continuous melody. It has a dexterous vocal range that includes whistles, coughs and croaks. Tuis bounce their songs and whistles back and forth across the treetops in sweet harmony. The more I listen, the more I think this bird must have an implanted voice box with recorded sounds of R2D2 from *Star Wars*. I instantly fall in love.

Birds are just about the only natural born citizens found in New Zealand's forests. There are no native mammals in the country, except the bat. Plenty of mammals have been introduced, like goat, deer and possums. Possums are hated in New Zealand. Someone in the 1800s thought it would be a good idea to establish fur trade in the country and introduced the rodents. Though just medium in size, the species has wreaked havoc on the country's ecosystems, particularly because they are omnivorous, killing off many of the endemic birds. There is a pest control system in place, but it can only make a small impact.

Still, as trampers, it is reassuring to know there is nothing in the forest that can kill us, especially no bear. But, it is also strange to be in the forest and not be on the lookout for wildlife. The squeaks of squirrels or chipmunks are noticeably absent.

A wood pigeon bursts out of some branches and gives me a fright. It makes me notice the trees, which have to be at least one hundred fifty feet tall, because I can't see their tops.

"Look babe, these are kauri trees!" I exclaim.

New Zealand has more than two thousand native plant species. Kauri are New Zealand's biggest Hollywood stars among the regional trees. Coniferous with narrow, leathery leaves, smooth bark and thick trunk girths, kauri can live for more than two thousand years.

These new sights and sounds really help distract us from the mud. We come up with a new phrase. Bloody mudtastic. I swear someone shipped in buckets of peanut butter to dump along the trail. The mud's quantity and depth could swallow a whole person. And it comes in colors besides brown, red and orange. The yellow and white make it a complete palette. I twist my trekking pole to release the suction of the mud and slog forward. Even postholing through snow is easier than this.

The mud and trail—or lack thereof—slow us down to a one mile-per-hour pace, thus plummeting our mood. The Northland forests are really where Te Araroa gnashes its teeth. This track seems like someone's bad idea of an obstacle course. Thick tree roots are hidden by slippery, knee-deep mud, which makes me fall and keeps undoing the velcro on Justin's gaiter protecting his boots, which he now agrees were a heartier footwear choice.

Justin tries not to let the mud get him or me down. "Some people get stuck in the mud, while some people walk through the mud, right?" he laughs at the mantra a fellow hiker friend taught us. Minor annoyances may be major obstacles, but we push through.

Over the birdsong, I hear someone speaking English. And not just English, American English. More proof we are not the only crazy ones.

We come upon a man in his early fifties on his cell phone at a clearing to the only vista that we've seen since we entered Herekino Forest. I spend some time scrutinizing the fresh-off-the-shelf look to the man's gear, then turn my gaze out to the ocean and nearby Ahipara while he wraps up his phone conversation. We come to learn Robert is an American, also attempting a thru hike of Te Araroa. He was hiking with his wife, but Ninety Mile Beach sabotaged her feet, so she is resting and he will meet up with her in KeriKeri, our next resupply stop.

We hike together for a few miles, exchanging stories of woe and agreeing Kiwi trails are not as user friendly as American trails.

"I've been carrying four liters of water," Robert tells

us. The thing about the Northland forests is there are no running streams, which is why I don't understand the bloody mudtastic state of the forest. I know Justin thinks four liters—which weighs more than eight pounds—is a major excess to carry, but I love water and understand why people fear running out.

We hit Taumatamahoe Summit, our planned camp spot for the evening. It is 4 P.M. and we've only done a little more than ten miles for the day, but I am happy to stop. Robert moves on. He has arranged a homestay with a local Kiwi and will finish Herekino Forest at a road crossing today. Similar to our encounter with Marilyne, we figure we'll see him down the trail sometime.

I wake a lot in the night, hearing the raucous protest of possums against our chosen campsite.

I emerge from my tent door to relieve myself and think it's a good opportunity to claim my first spotting of the Southern Hemisphere sky and its most distinct constellation, the Southern Cross. But, the clouds and the full moon have rendered the heavens starless tonight. Another night, perhaps; there will be plenty more.

The following morning, beautiful—albeit very loud—birdsong awakens me. Is it a kiwi? No, I'm once again hearing the schizophrenic tui, or R2D2. The dawn breeze carries the scent of the wet earth into our tent. It is only 5:06 A.M. With December upon us, early dawn and late dusk give us more than fourteen hours of daylight. Still, we won't be getting up and moving for at least another two hours; we are admittedly lazy morning people. I lay and soak up the first rays of sunlight filtering in through the trees and tent walls, warming me with an orange glow.

At 8:10 A.M., I am standing with my pack on, straps

tightened and buckled, ready to go. Justin is packing his bag in slow motion, it seems. My eyes laser into Justin's back, trying to will him to move faster. I adjust my watch. I tighten my gaiter. I rub my neck. I do anything to avoid the growing apprehension of the forest mud ahead of us. How would we ever complete this trail if we repeat our measly ten-mile progress from the previous day?

Justin is the go-with-the-flow half of our relationship; he thrives on uncertainty and worries about very little. On the other hand, I research everything I can in advance, analyze trail data and clearly communicate definitive plans to anyone who will listen. It's like the universe put us together to find the perfect balance—if we don't kill each other in the process. To be fair, during our decade-plus together, his influence has forced me to loosen up immensely and appreciate his relaxed manner. Twenty-four-year-old Patrice would set her alarm for 4:45 A.M. to go for her daily hike and be at her desk job by 7 A.M. Now at age thirty-six, I carry a different persona, but that doesn't mean Justin's wasted minutes and unhurried morning routine aren't completely unbothersome.

My other half finally fastens his chest strap and grabs his trekking poles, which is my green light to start leading us downhill out of the Herekino Forest. My watch shows 8:20 A.M.

Bright sunshine greets us as we exit the forest onto Diggers Valley Road. There is a large orange triangle marker pointing to the right. Upon closer inspection, there is a fading, hand-drawn black arrow pointing to the left, with a note under reading:

T.A. GO AHEAD. CHECK YOUR MAP IF YOU DON'T BELIEVE ME.

There is also a smiley face.

"What the fuck?" I blurt out.

Te Araroa has no guidebook, making navigation the trickiest part of the whole trek. Before we left the United States, I printed seventy-five pages front and back of trail notes superimposed on maps. To help prepare us for Te Araroa, I surfed the Internet absentmindedly scouring for clues about the trail. In August, I was surrounded by printed maps, several computer tabs open with various blogs and a 2013 print copy of *A Walking Guide To New Zealand's Long Trail Te Araroa*. Justin would look on and joke, "I'll just follow you." Logistics planning almost took the fun out of the whole trek.

Unfortunately, the trail notes and maps we carry leave a lot left to be desired.

We pull out our loose leaf "guidebook" for the fourth time of the day and analyze the map and trail notes together. Neither one of us is particularly good with orienteering. Without indicating a direction, our notes say to follow the "windy metal road." It looks gravel—not metal—to us, but we think nothing of it. Justin and I are also not the most decisive people. We exchange a lot of "whadda you thinks" before coming up with the best rationalization that not one of the twenty-five-plus hikers in front of us crossed out the handwritten note and arrow. We opt left.

Of course there are no orange markers on the road and after more than a mile of walking what is supposed to be less than a mile without seeing our turnoff, we decide we need to ask someone, or backtrack in the other direction. We also wonder if maybe we are on the wrong road. It is, afterall, still gravel and supposed to be metal, whatever that means.

I turn on the GPS option for my fancy Garmin Fenix watch. There is a line—presumably Te Araroa—and an arrow. For all I know, we could be in London. I curse myself for not signing up for that REI navigation course.

As luck would have it, a car comes in our direction. We flag the person down, show him our maps and the name of the forest we are supposed to be entering. He is very gracious, turning off his car and getting out to help us. However, he is slurring his words and the smell of beer cuts through the dusty cloud his car created. I'm not sure we should trust him any more than we trust handwritten notes on the trail signs. We send the man on his merry way.

Meltdowns are not worth the energy. And we both realize we're not going to die here. We backtrack. When we pass the culprit orange triangle, we slap duct tape over the instructions, including the happy face. Never a mistake, always a lesson.

Minutes later, we reach the marked entrance we should have come to an hour earlier.

As we are finishing up our late lunch, our French-Canadian connection, Marilyne, strolls in. Marilyne's vibrant soul lifts our dampened spirits and she is a welcoming sounding board to commiserate the forest and state of the trail thus far. We continue to talk as we walk the second gravel road together. Marilyne has never done other long-distance backpacking, so we bombard her with stories of easier—not necessarily better, that is to be determined—trails. Marilyne also introduces us to the app "iHikeGPS NZ." She explains it works on satellite and really hones in her location in relation to Te Araroa. We agree we should definitely download it the next time we are in a town with service or WiFi.

The three of us camp together at the beginning of Rataea Forest. Another day of sub-ten-mile progress in the books, not to mention our three-mile detour. We fall asleep listening to the animal kingdom around us.

I somehow sleep through the 5 A.M. wake-up cacophony the next morning. By 6:55 A.M., Marilyne has packed up her tent and is putting on her backpack. We say our goodbyes, again assuming we will see each other down the trail.

After the first few miles of the Rataea Forest, we agree the Herekino Forest was a Sunday stroll.

Kiwis insist on calling Herekino and Rataea "forests," but we have aptly renamed them "jungles." We keep our heads down, looking for disturbed mud and maybe even proof of Marilyne's boot prints. Once in a while, I look up searching for an orange triangle marker amongst the sea of green and brown and to make sure no tree branches threaten impalement.

Besides the mud, the Rataea Forest has some of the highest points in the Northland, so the forest is constantly pulling in storms from both the Pacific Ocean and Tasman Sea. With so much rain growing a dense forest and the fact that very few people go tramping in the Northland, there is an incredible amount of overgrowth to claw through. The unmaintained forest envelops mystery, with its vibrant canopy of Amazon-green-colored mosses, ferns and other native plant life. It is hard to remember this was more than a movie set from *Lord of the Rings*. It looks— and certainly feels—impenetrable.

Rataea is also the place I realize something else about

Kiwi trails. They either haven't discovered yet, or have something against, switchbacks. Instead of zig-zagging up the hill, reducing the elevation grade, the path sends us straight up on steep and slippery tracks. We are once again giving an elephant's effort at a snail's pace.

I dig my trekking pole into the mud and hoist myself up the near-vertical hill, only to be simultaneously strangled and tripped by a supple jack vine.

"This is inhumane! A sufferfest! It has to be a joke!" I whine. "This can't be the trail!"

Justin is too busy to share my misery because he is also being dragged backwards by the vines and slog.

After what seems like an eternity, I see an orange triangle hanging on a low branch like a Christmas ornament.

In a tone like a teenager who works at McDonald's and is super annoyed that someone has asked for extra ketchup, I mumble, "I see a trail marker."

A few minutes later, we reach orange triangle markers going in two different directions, as well as a handwritten note signifying that the left fork is correct. This seems eerily familiar. We waste more time being skeptical and indecisive, then go left, as it best matches our map, trail notes and compass direction. It stays well marked with orange triangle markers, so our confidence levels remain high.

Suddenly, the trail markers stop. We take out our trail notes and map for the tenth time of the day. The time we've traveled just doesn't match. We should have hit Makene Road by now. We backtrack to the last orange blaze, praying for a clue. Two hours later—with a lot of up and down searching along the trail—we are still on a witch hunt for trail markers and affirmation.

Justin throws his trekking pole at a tree. I talk Justin down from the ledge, but don't do a very good job. We are equally frustrated by the trail and we have to be careful of staying angry at it, instead of each other, even though we are the only objects capable of response.

I decide to check if my phone has a signal. I am thinking I could text Marilyne and see how far ahead she is or if she has insight.

Jackpot! I have one bar of service. It was a smart choice to purchase the two-month phone plan of two gigabytes of data, one hundred texts and one hundred minutes of call time from Vodafone in New Zealand. We are relying on it more than we ever thought we would.

I remember the app Marilyne described, iHikeGPS NZ. Instead of asking Justin and spending five minutes debating, I click "Buy App," agreeing to spend $9.99 on a little bit of sanity. I want to rely on something other than our joint gut feelings and the confusing trail notes and maps.

I fill Justin in on our plans as the app and area map downloads. I tap "my location" and a blue dot ensures us we are on Te Araroa.

We spend an equal amount of time cheering and cursing when we confirm we are on trail—despite the lack of blazes—and that we need to keep heading downhill.

That night, we catch up with the American, Robert, at Apple Dam, one of the rare established campsites on the trail. Again, we share woes of route finding.

"Did you see all the bee boxes today?" Robert asks. For a country with a small population of four million people, there are nearly five thousand beekeepers. We are in manuka tree territory, a native scrub tree that produces a honey with antibacterial properties, which explains the plethora of bee boxes around every corner today. Our trail notes read:

BUTTON UP AND WALK STEADY

I have a particular trepidation about buzzing flies with stingers. On our Appalachian Trail thru hike, an Asian Giant Hornet bit me in the corner of my eye. That insect was the size of my fist and the bite turned me into the character Sloth from *Goonies* for a week. I alter Te Araroa's trail notes to be safe.

BUTTON UP AND WALK BRISKLY

The next day, Justin, Robert and I hike most of the day together, dividing the load of the navigational challenges. It is the day we discover this trail is sometimes a choose-your-own-adventure. For nearly two miles, we follow Mangapukahukahu Stream and Waipapa River. And when I mean follow, I mean we are literally walking downstream in the waterways. Without any rain during the past eight days, the river is only ankle-deep, but this section is a gorge, so we have to remain mindful of the possibility of flash floods.

With my boots off and camp shoes on, the flow of crisp water offers some respite for my feet. The confetti-colored pebbles and stones underfoot are so well polished, it requires little focus and attention walking through the river. The sun glistening off the flow mesmerizes me and I declare this a good day on the trail.

There are a few bits where the river pools far too deep for wading, so the track leads us up and into the forest hills cloaked with young kauri, manuka and dracophyllum. Robert falls behind during the forest section and we agree to meet up at the same camp spot that night. Because of erosion, we negotiate single-foot wide paths and avoid precarious vertical drop offs. I twitch my nose. There is a rancid smell of fresh urine, bad enough that I pull my shirt collar to block my nostrils. I assume it is more rotting possum carcasses; our count is up to seven dead possums in traps for the day. I stop short. Wildlife! There are six mountain goats ahead on the trail. They must smell us, too, because they scatter just as soon as we spot them.

That night, we call it quits at Puketi Recreation Centre, an established Department of Conservation campground on the trail. You can drive into the campground, and many sites are already full, as it is 8 P.M. The campervan tourists eye us dubiously, speaking in whispers, seemingly trying to figure out how these two vagrants appeared out of nowhere.

Knowing Justin would want to assess every single campsite before deciding, I ignore the watchful eyes of the motorized travelers and plop down at the first picnic table I see. The last six miles of road walking leading to Puketi really made my dogs bark. As I peel off my sock, a toenail on my right foot comes with it. This one marks the second fallen soldier of the trip.

Justin tells me we should look for a suitable spot on the other side of the campground away from the RVs and I lag behind him as he marches from campsite to campsite.

"Whadda you think about this one?" He asks as he is kicking the grassy area, searching for roots.

Justin's pickiness for the perfect piece of camping real estate is a trait of his that pushes my buttons, like on speed dial. And I'm not sure why he asks my opinion every time. He knows I could care less and always opt for the path of least resistance, but still feels the need to discuss. It's as if asking out loud validates his strong opinion, which is masked by his indecisiveness.

I drop my backpack and boots as my answer. I could camp alongside a live rock concert right now and sleep for days.

As Justin slurps the last noodle of our Pad Thai dehydrated meal, Robert limps into camp. It is his fiftieth birthday and I break out our dehydrated blueberry cheesecake in celebration.

We all fall asleep under the spotlight of the full moon above.

On day nine, our walk into KeriKeri is a combination of private farmland and urban pathways, but we are once again mystified by the navigation.

Scanning the rural landscape, there are no orange markers—or any markers for that matter. The hundreds of cow and sheep eye us benevolently. As soon as we come within twenty feet of the sheep, they barrel into sprint mode using their spindle-like legs, shouting sporadic cheers of "BAAAAH" all the way up the rolling hills. Once they are a safe distance from the intruders, they herd themselves into a tight circle. The cows, on the other hand, continue to chew on their verdant grass unperturbed and occasionally pee and poop.

Inevitably, we end up on the wrong part of the property, right about when a farmer is herding one thousand sheep from one paddock to another. We hug the fence line as much as possible to give the farm animals a wide berth, as the border collies nip at sheeps' hooves. The farmer graciously steers us back to the trail—like we are sheep—saying this is not the first time he's seen hikers go off course.

I spot a few pukeko milling about the swampy area at the bottom of the farmland. The native birds' brilliant blue breasts and conical red beaks offer a stark contrast to the yellow and green grasslands.

We enter a second patch of farmland, this one colonnaded with orange markers. Some Department of Conservation workers are blazing the farm track. I hesitate to ask about the tight budget for trail markers in the previous section and just thank them profusely for their work. Unlike trails in America, which have large networks of volunteers, Te Araroa is still growing and falls under the responsibility of two government agencies— Department of Conservation and Te Araroa Trust. The Department of Conservation is a large organization. However, its multiple responsibilities puts Te Araroa lower on the priority list. The Trust is solely dedicated to the trail, although it is a small organization and has to focus more on land negotiations and community relations rather than trail maintenance.

Near the end of the farm track, we encounter new obstacles: barbed wire and electric fencing. In spite of my yoga practice, my balance is pitiful, so I get electrocuted four times by the end of the day. Justin's count is zero.

We arrive in KeriKeri late in the day. KeriKeri is the first populated town we've walked through and the sense of New Zealand history is palpable. The surrounding area was the scene of the most significant event in the country's history—the signing of the Treaty of Waitangi between the British Crown and the aboriginal Maori tribes on Feb. 6, 1840, resulting in British sovereignty over New Zealand.

On the town's urban pathway, we meet Matt, out for a

jog. An armchair tramper, he is keen to hear more about our adventures and offers to buy us a cold drink at Pear Tree Café, the end of the path. I have been dreaming about pineapple juice, and am happy to see it on the menu.

Following our short exchange of adventures with Matt, we settle in at Hone Heke Hostel on the outskirts of KeriKeri and start our laundry right away. Doing laundry is a bit of a chore in New Zealand, as they are very conscious about energy usage and hardly anyone has dryers. I am not opposed to line drying clothes, but it just means we need to get started on laundry right away to allot enough time for the drying process. We decide on shorter miles tomorrow so we can take care of town duties in the morning—drying laundry, resupply, blog updates and phone calls to home.

Two hours later, Robert joins us at the hostel, reuniting with his wife, who is still not excited about getting back on the trail. Most of the other hostel guests are working visa international tourists picking fruit for the season.

The next morning, I wake not knowing where I am. Occupational hazard, really.

After thru hiking the Appalachian Trail in 2011, we made a conscious and bold decision not to return to the societal norm of status quo life. Even though we both had thriving careers we loved—Justin working in municipal parks and recreation and I in medical writing—we wanted to be more than weekend warriors. We didn't quite know what it meant at the time, but we knew we wanted to carve out more time for outdoor adventures. What we organically created was a "life less ordinary."

We pieced together work in the hospitality and

outdoor industries, many times seasonal and alongside each other. Simulating a life of modern-day nomads, we moved around a lot, made important connections and encountered incredibly good fortune. Our jobs included managing a hiker hostel on the Appalachian Trail, a remote tipi bed and breakfast in Oregon and a gear-related speaking tour for *Backpacker Magazine*. During the 150 days we lived on the road for *Backpacker* in 2013, we slept in at least 75 different locations.

I lay there in another new bed thinking about the mud, the electrocution, the getting lost, the blisters. Has it only been ten days on Te Araroa? There seems to be no gentle break-in period on Te Araroa. New Zealand is into extreme sports and this is an extreme trail. Every day could be harder than the last. Someone left a comment on our most recent blog post asking, "When are you going to be in the enjoyable parts of this hike?"

But I've endured hard things in my life. I ran two half marathons. I walked the Appalachian Trail in 141 days. I climbed most of the state's highest peaks. I survived two blood clots in my lung. I ate my mom's runny scrambled eggs when I didn't think I could stomach them. This is just one more hard thing I seem to long for.

One step at a time, I remind myself. When we hike long distances, we never look at the big picture. It would scare us too much. We approach the trail in bite-size goals. In fact, it wasn't until the last seventy miles of the Appalachian Trail that we said emphatically that we were finishing. I should know that the first few weeks of any thru hike are always going to suck.

The main reason I truly want to be here: trail life is simple. Everyone should experience life at this slow of a pace. Work obligations, the distractions of technology and so many other things make life pass without noticing. And for a marriage, there aren't many things to argue about on trail as there are in the real world, like who's going to scoop cat poop from the litter box, schedule the oil change and put the dishes away. Trail life is freeing; the division of labor in camp chores has very little fuss.

However, even for us—the ones with the coveted non-traditional life—we needed this reset. We might have created an idyllic life on paper, but burning through multiple jobs in new locations takes a serious hustle. We were chasing our vagabond dream, although being slammed up to the reality of living it was a different story. We escaped the traditional forty-hour workweek, and sometimes ended up working eighty hours in a week.

Given our individual strengths and personalities, my planner role for this life hung on me like a superpower—it was both a blessing and curse. My anxiety is the reason we don't end up at a closed campground while living on the road, because I obsess over details. However, being the keeper of all life's logistical details, such as passwords, paperwork and photos, exhausted me these last four years. In fact, I sometimes felt like our life was more complicated and chaotic than a status quo one. Like beads on a necklace, I had been unknowingly collecting feelings of resentment.

So I'll take the lost toenails, route-finding and weather right now, because with it comes a fresh breeze kissing my cheeks, the sun's rays hugging me, the lullaby of the rustling leaves and birdsong and the smell of the Earth. Navigating the dirt and rocks one step at a time awards me with the deepest connection with my surroundings I can get.

One hundred more miles. Not two thousand more miles. Just one hundred. I can do that.

I sit up to start the process all over again.

| 3 |

Trail Family
Days 10-15: 96.1 miles

By noon, we leave Robert with his wife behind in KeriKeri and gain a new hiking mate, Matteo, who was also staying at Hone Heke Hostel. Matteo is a twenty-something Italian man whose heart is full of wonder, determination and loyalty. His accent is as thick as his long, black hair.

"Do you mind very much," he speaks slowly and deliberately, "if I camp with you tonight?"

We welcome the suggestion and he says "Beautiful. Thankyouverymuch."

Besides our Italian stallion, Matteo, we reunite on trail with the French Canadian, Marilyne. For the ensuing six days, the four of us travel together, with the confidence of an international pack of wolves, hungry for the trail.

Now on the eastern coast of New Zealand, our walking affords postcard vistas of the Bay of Islands and the Pacific

Ocean around every corner. Through the fairyland of 144 undeveloped islands off the country's eastern coast, our eyes are drawn like magnets to the aqua sea and long sandy beaches hugged by hillsides, draped in multiple hues of green. Lining the sidewalks we follow, the pohutukawa trees have blossomed with bushy red flowers, offering a triple blessing of shade, birdsong and beauty. On top of all that, there are seriously sublime patches of tent real estate available for freedom camping. Justin no longer has to try so hard. The incredible stretch of clear weather translates to consecutive nights under a carpet of sparkling diamonds.

One of those great camp spots is Mt. Bledisloe. When we stumble upon the scenic picnic area—which was not listed in our trail notes as anything special—we are gobsmacked by the summit looking six hundred feet below over a large swathe of perfectly manicured lawns disappearing into the limitless ocean.

We scour the land for "No Camping" signs, but there are none. In an effort to leave less of a trace, the four of us plan to set up our tents post-sunset. Being there is road access and a car park just down the hill, this is a conscious effort to consider our impact on the multiple drive-in day visitors, aiming to disturb the scene as little as possible.

The seven principles of Leave No Trace—including Be Considerate of Other Visitors—are near and dear to Justin and I. Leave No Trace is a national nonprofit in the United States, and its wide network of volunteers help spread awareness on how to enjoy the outdoors responsibly through the seven principles.

In 2014, we applied for a job with Leave No Trace to be a part of their Traveling Trainer Teams. The job put teams on the road around the United States, educating the masses about preserving our natural environment through Leave No Trace principles. In our minds, we are made for this role. When we made it to the interview round, but not beyond, we vowed to reapply time and time again until we secured the job.

In order to improve our chances for the 2015 application, we became Leave No Trace Master Educators, which involved taking a five-day certification course on ways to educate others about taking care of nature responsibly. My sister, who is not at all into the outdoors, told me she didn't understand how these lessons could take five days to teach. "Isn't it simple?" she joked. "Bury your poop. The end." But, it was more about the teaching methods to effectively relay the messages across varying audiences. As international travelers in New Zealand, we know we could help spread Leave No Trace guidelines beyond the United States.

Matteo, Marilyne, Justin and I are huddled together off to the side of the picnic area cooking dinner.

"Shit," Matteo groans. I see his cous cous has spilled from his pot. I realize this is a teachable Leave No Trace moment when he starts scooping up the food and chucking it into the forest.

"Um, Matteo, you probably need to gather the mess into a garbage baggie and take it with you," I look at Justin for support.

"But why?" Matteo asks. "The animals will eat it, no?"

"They would," Justin instructs. "But, it's not good for them. It could make them sick or they may start to depend on people food. Plus, if someone sees the mess of food, that's not good for the reputation of TA hikers."

"Sorry to be on top of you about this," I continue. "It's just one of the ways we can keep this beautiful."

"No, I understand," Matteo says, trying to pick up every last scrap. "Thankyouverymuch for teaching me."

After dinner, Marilyne and I are sitting on the bench, discussing the trail notes for the upcoming section. Justin and Matteo are within earshot, but consumed in their own conversation about the pros and cons of a butane camping stove versus an alcohol stove. A group of four eloquently dressed adults equipped with fancy cameras and tripods walk up the pathway. Marilyne and I offer up the park bench, as it is the best viewpoint.

"Would it bother you if she took her clothes off?" the woman with the biggest camera asks, pointing to a slender lady standing beside to her. The two men in the group are setting up the tripods and video cameras at varying angles.

I am happy Marilyne answers "no" promptly and nonchalantly because I am still processing if I heard right about clothes coming off. Marilyne and I step back toward the boys. I am suddenly very conscious about my body odor and take two more steps away from them.

The four of us are like teenagers watching porn for the first time, drool and all. The main character in this movie sensually unties her flowing red dress, slipping it over her head and throwing it off to the side like it is a dirty tissue. The muse has no bra on and from my angle, I see her aroused right nipple. She is wearing a red thong. Sitting on the top part of the park bench with her shoulders and spine tall, she drinks in the last bits of sunlight. She slowly reaches both arms toward the sky, sliding the backside of her left hand down her chest back to her side. Her other arm follows. She spends a few moments weaving and twirling her fingers through her long, auburn mane. The dusk lowlight is adding a halo around her. Her creamy white buttocks form a heart shape, peeking up over the wood. I shift my weight, wondering how that position could be comfortable and if she is getting any splinters down under.

Minutes later—or maybe hours for all we know—the quartet pack up all their equipment and the model saunters off, fully dressed again. They holler back "cheers" and "thank you," as if they are afterthoughts.

"Deed that jest rally happen?" Matteo asks.

Our next few days are filled with some uninspiring road walking and another short riverwalk as we navigate through land owned by the Maori. New Zealand's indigenous people now only make up fifteen percent of the entire country's population.

"Tough day," I harrumph to Marilyne, throwing down my bag at our makeshift campsite.

"Yeah," she agrees. "Matteo tried to find a trail through the woods, but I don't think that worked because I caught up to him as he was splashing through the river. He put up his hands and said, 'fuckin trail' and moved on through the water."

"Oh," I furrowed my brow. "We stopped and took off our boots to do all the crossings."

"What? That's crazy!"

"We always do that when we can't rock hop. We change into our camp shoes. We like that much better." I scratch my dozens of sandfly bites on my ankles. Sandflies are New Zealand's famous blood-sucking insects. They are small black flies, as tiny as gnats, that breed near water and won't kill you, but are maddeningly annoying.

"But what will you do when we are crossing twenty rivers and braids in one day on the South Island? And what about the eels?"

I seriously hope Justin didn't hear the part about the eels. He is an avid outdoorsman, but certain things like snakes and eels give him the shudders. As for the reference to the upcoming crossings, I didn't answer Marilyne because I honestly didn't know we would be making that many water crossings. I must have glazed over it in my research.

"Where is Matteo?" I ask, trying to change the subject.

"Not sure. Guess he didn't stop here and moved on."

The roadside campsite riddled with trash isn't ideal, but it works for our two tents. Matteo's would never have fit anyway. We call his tent "the palace." The rain starts and the three of us retire to our shelters.

We catch back up to Matteo at Wananaki Holiday Park, run by Matthew and Tracy, who are delighted to accommodate hikers overnight and even offer a discount. Over an ice cream treat provided by Tracy, Matthew regales us with stories of the hikers who have stayed with them this year. We are numbers eighty-three and eighty-four. The overgrown trail we encountered in the four forests made it seem like no one had been there in decades, let alone eighty hikers in the preceding weeks.

Matthew's enthusiasm for hosting hikers reminds us of our year managing Bears Den Trail Center and Hostel on the Appalachian Trail, our first "life less ordinary" gig. Bears Den had thirty-five beds in the drop-in hostel, plus a campground. Working in the hospitality business taught us that it's actually not a job; it's a lifestyle. Because as a job, there is nothing worse if you consider how many hours you work and how many times you have to clean a toilet. But as a lifestyle, there is nothing better considering all the people you will meet and memories you will collect. Unfortunately, we will later learn that Matthew passed away in 2016.

The road walking continues the following day, but the rain lets up. The roadkill count for possums is up to four by noon. On the plus side, our pace hits three miles per hour and we see more and more of Kiwi culture. Bare-chested and barefooted, everyone waves on the streets. Their mailboxes, or letterboxes as Kiwis call them, are nothing short of wacky. We see recycled microwaves, a life-sized dragon and a boat engine. It keeps things interesting for us and I snap photos around every new bend.

On December 9, the four of us road walk and reunite at Hilton's house. Hilton and his wife own a bed and breakfast in Ngunguru and he allows Te Araroa trampers to camp on his lawn in exchange for a koha (Maori word for donation).

With no guests at the B&B that evening, Hilton invites us inside for a cuppa tea.

Hilton is a great resource about New Zealand and even Te Araroa. I finally ask him my burning question about metaled roads. We have now seen this term used in our trail notes several times, along with "paper roads" and "unsealed roads."

"Mital," he explains in his Kiwi accent, "or unsealed roads are going to be whot you know as dirt or gravel roads. Sealed roads are paved."

"Wow," I nod my head. "You have instantly demystified us."

"Have you guys tried Whittaker's chocolate?" he asks. The four of us shake our heads no. Chocolate is my kryptonite, so both my interest and taste buds are piqued.

He pulls out an unopened half-pound bar of Whittaker's Milk Chocolate. I can't help but lick my lips.

Hilton goes into a five-minute soliloquy about how the Kiwi brand of Whittaker's is the best chocolate we will find in all of New Zealand, really the whole world. The bar of unopened chocolate sits in the middle of the table, taunting us.

"Definitely get your hands on some chocolate," he finishes, putting the chocolate back in his cabinet. Silently, I debate if I should offer him money for the bar of chocolate that I so desperately want now. I talk myself out of being so bold, but make a mental note to buy Whittaker's at the very next chance.

Leaving Hilton's the subsequent morning, we are faced with more sealed road walking in the rain. I had read about a number of hikers hitchhiking the road portions in this section. Justin, Marilyne and Matteo have no interest in skipping any of the trail. I do my best to convince Justin that hitching the initial six miles of road walking today is a good idea for my sanity, and my feet, which have started screaming at me again. My purist husband concedes, as long as I promise not to make this a daily habit.

A nice Kiwi picks us up within five minutes and we blow by Marilyne, then Matteo, both walking with their heads down on the pavement in the pouring rain.

We agree we dodged a nice bullet as our ride drops us off just in time for the rain to slow to a slight drizzle. We enter the Mackerel Forest Track and realize we are dead wrong. A field of head-height pampas grass, newly doused with rainfall, stands in our way. We see orange triangle markers on the trees, but a trail underfoot? Not visible to the human eye. The pampas grass may look soft, but as we bash our way through the bush, its razor-sharp edges do a wonderful job of slicing up our exposed arms like a ninth-grade dissection project gone wrong. As a bonus on this obstacle course, the blades hide streams and deep mud pits.

I trip for the sixth time today, while Justin belts out his twentieth sneeze. When we exit the forest—earlier confidence fully busted—we are both soaked from head to toe. Justin is also covered with hives, thanks to his seasonal allergies.

As if our day could not deteriorate anymore, we square off against our first of many estuary crossings, where the river meets the sea. Te Araroa is full of major logistical challenges. Earlier in the week, we hired a boat taxi when the trail dumped us into Waikare Inlet, an eight-mile water crossing. Today's Taiharuru Estuary is feasible to cross at low tide, however, the sign reads:

LOW TIDE 5:30 P.M. TODAY

Justin's wry face as he glances at his watch says it all. It is 1 P.M. He sticks a branch in the sand at the water line and we take out our cheese, salami and crackers for our long lunch break. The water lashes the sand and retreats for an hour. Plovers and oystercatchers come and go, poking at the wet sand for delicious matter to bring back to their nests. I appreciate that Justin's face explosions have subsided temporarily, but the waiting drives me mad.

"The trail notes say 'firmer sand can be found away from the mangroves, which line the shoreline.'" I look at Justin's branch in the sand. The water line is now ten feet away. "The sign says the crossing should only take an hour. The notes warn it could be muddy, but it just can't be any worse than what we've been through."

At 2:30 P.M., our patience expires. At first, we travel easily. Like monkeys, we climb up and over the mangrove trees' seemingly chaotic root systems to avoid walking in the mud. At the intersection of land and sea, these salt-tolerant trees survive hostile coastal conditions and offer as much of a nursery for fish as they do for birds and insects. But then, the clusters of mangroves become too thick to travel through safely.

On one side of the mangrove forest is the still-waning estuary. On the other side is a fence line, presumably marking private property. We shoot for the water side first. Although it looks dry and cracked, the waterlogged mud underneath sucks us down like quicksand.

"Go back!" I yelp. By this time, it is 4 P.M. and we have traveled ten percent of the distance we need to.

We heave our backpacks and ourselves over the welded wire fence. We share the paddock with about fifteen heifers. Typically, the cows are content to the point of smugness. But today, these ladies want to nuzzle our backpacks. They are snorting and revealing their sinister set of enormous protruding piano keys. I interpret this as skyrocketing bovine stress. We jump quickly to the adjoining paddock, which contains a dozen horses, whose thundering hooves, powerful limbs and bulging nostrils are heading straight toward us.

"Run!" Justin howls.

My heart feels like it doesn't have enough room in its ribcage.

We vault another fence hastily to exit the horse

territory. This paddock is empty, so we both take the opportunity to normalize our heart rhythm.

At 4:45 P.M., we exit the private property to face the rest of the crossing. It is muddy, but completely doable.

Across the sloppy estuary, we schlepp along on the metaled roads the rest of the way to a beautiful camp spot overlooking Ocean Beach.

As soon as we set up the tent, Justin collapses inside. Our foolhardy tide mishap exhausted us both mentally and physically, but he is especially plagued. Crohn's goes hand in hand with all sorts of other chronic health manifestations, including a higher risk of seasonal allergies. We found that Justin can sometimes dodge the local area allergens moving around as much as we do, but New Zealand seems to be the worst he's ever had. A speckled mass of welts still covers his legs and he simply cannot stop sneezing.

"I feel like I'm gonna die," he moans.

I realize that I tucked five allergy pills into our first aid kit at the last minute before leaving the United States in a moment of rare responsibility. I hand Justin two to take.

"We'll have to get you more on our next town stop, but maybe this will give you some relief."

While Justin is silently dying beside me, I turn on my phone. A text from Robert and Matteo pops up.

Robert's reads, "My wife and I decided to rent a car and explore the country. Good luck on the trail!" Yeah, I hear ya Robert.

Matteo's reads, "hi guys at kilometer 375 where are you."

I pop my head out of the tent, scanning the farmland, realizing we are also at kilometer 375. I climb out of the tent to get a better look and still see no sign of Matteo.

"What are you doing?" Justin grumbles.

"Matteo texted us and said he is camped here, but I don't see him."

"What? Really?"

I hear rustling and somehow Justin musters enough strength to emerge from the tent.

We call out Matteo's name together.

"I'll go check closer to the trail," Justin suggests.

I grab my phone and send a text to Matteo telling him we are here too and asking where exactly he is.

I see Justin running back over toward me.

"I found him! And if you think our view is killer here, wait til you see where he is camped!"

We pull out the tent stakes and Justin—who now has the energy of a bull—heaves the tent above his head, with the sleeping pads and bags still inside.

"I've got this if you get our backpacks and boots."

Happily, we reunite with Matteo perched on a cliff overlooking the ocean. Like yolk seeping out of an egg, the sun dips below the horizon.

"You guys iz crazy. I saw you crossing the estuary and it did not look fun," Matteo tells us he met a nice gentleman at the estuary start, right at 3:30 P.M. This stranger invited him in to enjoy tea and biscuits while waiting for low tide.

Matteo throws his hands up, saying, "fuckin trail." We all laugh.

| 4 |

The Rainy Northland
Days 16-21: 73.2 miles

We wake to rain. I peek out of the tent around 7 A.M. and see Marilyne heading down the trail to the beach. She camped before the estuary to ensure a lower-tide morning crossing—proving our trail friends have more patience than us. She is too far away for me to yell over the swirling wind.

"We have to get moving," I nudge Sleeping Beauty. "Low tide on the beach is 10:30 A.M." I am forever jaded by the tides and won't take any chances.

Matteo is still in his tent mansion enjoying breakfast as we tighten our hip belts.

"We'll see you later," I offer and he responds with his typical, "have a nice day."

The ocean is its turbulent self, with brigades of whitecaps marching in a line. It is clear we have been smacked with a new pressure system and the rain continues on and off. Thank God none of us are made of sugar. We walk the wet, packed sand, noticing the sea creatures close to the surface, waiting for the water to return. As high tide approaches, the stretches of firm sand give way to softer surfaces closer to the dunes.

At an empty beach car park, we find a kiosk with an overhang, giving shelter from the downpour. We cook up a soup for lunch. Only on days like this when the cold eats deep into our bodies do we eat hot lunches. I immediately welcome the warmth spreading throughout my body and can continue on in the rain.

Before entering the ensuing coastal forest section, I search through the low-lying fog creeping unevenly along the shoreline. There is no sign of Matteo.

The track climbs steeply to a World War II naval radar station. At this point, I am more interested in the shelter the remaining structure is providing than the history behind it. If it weren't for the petrichor that rose from the wet earth, I could close my eyes and imagine we were not walking in the rain. There are supposed to be magnificent coastal panoramas in this region, but the fog is so thick we are looking at the views through wax paper.

The trail continues to follow the ridge to Mount Lion. The trail markers disappear and we question the map and notes for the first time today. There is a clear path that leads to some boulders. It looks daunting. Justin cautiously scrambles up in hopes of finding a marker. I break out in a sweat for the first time today as I watch him struggle to get stable footing negotiating the wet rocks. He disappears out of sight up and over the rocky and forbidding barricade. I retrace my steps to the last orange triangle and survey the scene again through the raindrops. I see nothing but the trail we are on.

Justin comes back down with bad news.

"No orange marker," he reports. "And it's really dicey up there. If I am nervous, you're gonna have a heart attack."

Deflated, we alternate uneasy glances between the trail notes, the iHikeGPS NZ app on the phone and the trees around. If only Matteo would stroll up in that moment to save us, or commiserate with us.

"Let me go back up there and look again," Justin proposes. We have no choice, really.

In the meantime, I go "off trail." Then, I spot it—a turnoff obscured in the darkness of the rainstorm and an orange marker veiled by the tree canopy.

I clamor up the first boulder and bellow to Justin.

No response.

I howl again. I can hear the echo of waves lapping below. My shaking legs prohibit me from climbing any higher.

Moments later, Justin peers over a high boulder and receives my positive news.

Once on dependable footing, he tells me it was downright precarious up there. We laugh nervously, knowing we had narrowly evaded tragedy.

The rain slows to a stop as we descend into Urquharts Bay. Matteo finally catches up and we soak up the sunshine and swap weathered stories before we head into the village. The planner in me has been dreading this section. Urquharts Bay is not really a town. There are no services. The population might be 150 people. What's worse, the trail ends here at the large estuary—one no one can cross via foot—and picks up across the water at Mardsen Point.

Our trail notes simply say:

LOOK OUT FOR A BOAT TO TAKE YOU ACROSS THE
CHANNEL

Another piece reads:

FISHING ENTHUSIASTS TEND TO DEPART EARLY
MORNING OR EVENING ACROSS THE HARBOR

The trail rumors about "hitching a ride with a local fisherman" chronicle tales of people sleeping on the docks and begging fishermen for a ride at 5 A.M. It is 4 P.M., so I feel confident we have our timing right at least. I text Marilyne to see how she fared. Her plans were to hitch the long car ride to Whangarei to pick up a mail drop and stay the night, then hitch to the other side at Mardsen Point. She tells me she caught a car ride no problem and wished us good luck.

The three of us mosey on the sidewalks past houses and boat docks. We see a man coming toward us walking a dog.

"Hi!" Justin slows as we approach him. "Is there any chance you have a boat and would be willing to take us across the bay? We would be willing to pay you."

He smiles politely, but says he has no boat. I am glad Justin doesn't bother asking him about sleeping on his lawn for the night; I am already feeling flustered by our request.

Justin spots a woman walking toward us across the street and launches into a similar plea. She responds with a maybe, but inquires more about us and our hike.

"Well," she smiles. "I do hev a boat and my son can take you across in the morning." As if things couldn't get better, she assures, "you can also sleep on my dad's lown tonight, I reckon."

Even though I had been chilled all day, a warm feeling washes over me.

The woman directs us to her dad's place and Doug welcomes us with open arms. He has a beautiful lawn spot with bay views for camping and an indoor toilet for us to use in his art studio. I would have loved a shower, but beggars can't be choosers and we are planning to stay in a hostel the following night in Waipu, so I can wait one more day.

Doug is retired and recently lost his wife. He started offering his lawn to hikers this year and has enjoyed their company.

"One day," he narrates over hot tea, "I started noticing some young people wolking down our streets with big beckpacks and ski poles. No one in the village knew this long-distance path was coming through." Without a ferry service, Doug hopes the Te Araroa Trust sets up a more formal system for hikers spilling into Urquharts Bay.

The next morning at high tide, Doug's grandson, Lewis, takes us across the bay. With four people and three backpacks crammed in the dinghy, it takes thirty minutes to go less than ten miles. At one shallow point, Lewis jumps out to push the boat across. The kindness of these Kiwis never ceases to amaze me. We force him to take $15 as a thank you.

On the other shore, we battle through the soft sand beach walking. Today's miles include a ping-pong match between beach and road waking. It is cloudy and hovering around fifty degrees, but the rain seems to be holding off. I take pleasure in the fact that we will be passing a town on the road shortly.

"Matteo, we are going to get an early lunch up ahead

in Ruakaka if you want to join us," I suggest.

He strokes his chin and responds, "I will not get lunch. But I will take a coffee. I am stopping here for a break. You go. I catch up."

The rain resumes as we are finishing our lunch. We leave Matteo with his coffee and hit the road-to-beach combination again.

By the end of our day, we are quite a sight walking into Waipu, with blue-tinted lips and dark-circled eyes peering out from our shroud of dirt-covered rain gear. When we finally peel off our layers at Waipu Wanderers Hostel, we discover our skin resembles shriveled raisins.

Hot showers and a delicious meal from Waipu Pizza Barn do well to buoy our spirits.

The torrent and cyclone pound all night and are still doing so Sunday morning. If I didn't know any better, I would have thought someone was speed dumping buckets of water outside.

We text back and forth with Matteo and Marilyne to tell them we have the entire hostel to ourselves and they should come join us. They are both staying outside of town at the holiday park campground. Marilyn would have come, but knew Matteo was on a stricter budget than all of us. The camp host felt so bad, she let Matteo sleep in the laundry room and Marilyn in the kitchen space out of the rain and cold. They plan to stay another night given the horrendous conditions.

We pitch the idea of work for stay to Steve, the owner of Waipu Wanderers Hostel, and he agrees. "Work for stay" is a common win-win hospitality term; in exchange for a free night to maintain our middle-of-the-road lodging budget, we give the hostel a deep clean. December

14th serves as a nice, unexpected zero day—our first—with FaceTime calls to home and TV watching as the squall continued outside. Steve gifted us an abandoned hiker resupply box. This person mailed himself a box full of food for the next section, but called Steve to say he was injured on day four and would not be coming through and could pass the supplies onto another hiker. Picking through the contents was like opening Christmas gifts. We left a few items for future trampers, but snagged the dried mangoes, dehydrated mushrooms, packet of coconut milk and dan dan noodles.

With a dodgy seven-day forecast hot on our heels Monday morning, we grudgingly decide we can't take a second zero. Matteo and Marilyne agree. We plan to meet up tonight in the next town, Mangawhai. There is a guy who lets hikers sleep in his house for a small koha and we make those arrangements.

I look up tide times for the one-mile beach section we will encounter right before Mangawhai and read low tide to be at 2:48 P.M. Based on that, we dilly-dally a little longer at Waipu Wanderers. It is spitting fat, cold rain-drops when we ring Steve's doorbell to say goodbye and thanks. He and his wife come to the door in their bath-robes and tea in hand. I am immediately second guessing our decision when they ask if we are sure we won't stay longer.

The first five miles is full-on pavement pounding. The rain feels like tiny ice cubes falling from the sky. I zip up my rain jacket as high as it can go and tighten my hood.

Within a few hours, we hit the farm from where we will access Mangawhai Cliffs. We pass a farmer and ask if we will be safe up on the cliffs given the hurricane-force storm surrounding us.

"The wind is blowing from the wist, so you'll be blown into the cliffs instade of off!" he informs cheerfully.

Climbing up my first stile of the day to enter the farmland, the sign catches my eye.

WARNING: LIVESTOCK INCLUDING BULLS, ELECTRIC FENCES, POISON, TRAPS.

STRAY DOGS WILL BE SHOT.

The wind howls, as if it is sharing stories with the farm animals. With every sixty mile-per-hour gust, I clutch my trekking poles like one does on a subway car to stay upright. This happens every forty seconds or so. Even the sheep are hunkering down under trees. I shout to Justin about waiting to find a spot for a lunch break, but the wind eats most of my words.

As soon as we find a sheltered place nearly at the top of the farm hill, we stop for lunch, famished as it is already 1 P.M. and it was futile to stop earlier in the wind. The air is calm and the rain does not reach us through the umbrella of cabbage and gum trees.

"Let's take a nice long break here before being battered along the cliffs, as well as on the beach walk that follows." I can tell Justin likes my suggestion because he almost completely unpacks his bag.

As Justin preps our tuna tortilla wraps, I turn on my phone to see a text from Marilyne at 12:15 P.M. saying she was at kilometer 442.5. I reply:

"1 P.M. We are at 441.5. You must be on the beach by now. How were the winds on the cliffs?? They were quite bad coming up here. Are we going to survive???"

Justin takes a bite of his tuna wrap, but most of it falls in his growing beard.

At 1:20 P.M., Marilyne replies.

"Hurry, high tide is coming. Be careful between 445K and 446K because of this. I'm at 446 and relieved to be done."

Thinking she is wrong about high tide, I check my app again. 2:48 P.M. is high tide, not low tide as I originally thought.

"We gotta go," I shriek, stuffing my last bite in my mouth. "I had my low tide time mixed up with my high tide time!"

We dash our way through Mangawhai Cliffs. It is blowing a fierce gale. I want to capture the intense beauty of the rocky headlands we are traversing, but also to catch my breath from the pace we are sustaining, I stop to take a picture and call to Justin to pose. Reluctantly, he does so, but races on before I tuck the iPhone back into my hip belt pocket.

Down off the cliffs and at the beach, we watch as our already narrow path diminishes with every thunderous swell breaking against the vertical rock dwellings. Occasional rock pancakes poke up above the frothy fingers of the Pacific Ocean, offering us safe spots to wait out the sea surge.

"Are you going to be okay with this?" Justin asks emphatically, while keeping his gaze on the wave patterns.

"What choice do we have?" I look gravely toward the road that pierces the cliffs. "I can't tell from the map how far out of the way this road goes, but I'm guessing it's close to ten miles. The beach is only one mile. I'll just follow your lead again."

Justin counts to three for us to run together onto the first safety islet. The slab is high enough that the ocean spray barely reaches the top where we are standing, but it is slick from the rainfall. I hear the evil, heavy waves in my left ear.

"Ready?" Justin looks at me for the nod of approval. He counts to three again and we run to the next closest flat rock. We repeat this pattern five or six times and I still can't see land around the towering cliff walls. My legs are quivering like a bowl of jello. I silently chastise myself for pushing to take the shorter route again. We could have also waited an hour or two for the tide to turn. Just when I am going to have to talk myself out of a panic attack, a large beach comes into view. There are people calmly frolicking about. Safety is within a few more mad rushes from the surf.

"That wasn't so bad," Justin declares valiantly. I ignore his disregard and make a beeline for the public restroom up at the car park before my nervous bowls explode.

As we are refilling our water at the drinking fountain, a woman comes up to us to say how fearful she was watching us negotiate the wild seas. I try to dissolve the look of terror on my face to reassure her, but it seems to be poured in concrete. She asks more about our journey and offers to give us a ride into Mangawhai. We politely decline, though I think she was slightly baffled when we explain it is part of the trail and we want to do it.

We have just a short three-mile road walk to Mangawhai. Being it is the evening hustle, there are hordes of people out and about stopping to talk to us. Everyone is talking about the liquid sunshine; they say the consecutive days of rain are an anomaly for New Zealand. Good for farming, bad for hikers.

Closer to our destination, a young fellow chats with us

on his evening walk. Paul is an adventurer himself, traveling the globe for work, but holding down roots in Mangawhai.

"Well good an ya. You must be bushed. I hev space for you to stay at my place, would you fancy staying thar?" Paul graciously offers.

"That's awfully nice of you, but we've made arrangements to stay with a man named Alan in town," Justin responds.

"Alan's a good ole bloke. No worries. Keep those arrangements, but come by for a bare end biscuits later tonight."

Justin sheepishly asks if we can bring two friends, knowing we'd want to invite Marilyne and Matteo.

"Of course bro. It's a go."

Later in the evening, we enjoy a beer and biscuits (apparently the Kiwi word for cookies) with Paul, who convinces Matteo—who hadn't made arrangements to stay at Alan's—to stay at his house instead. Knowing we have another tide-dependent day with three river crossings along the ten-mile section of beach, we keep it to a short gathering to anticipate an early start on Tuesday. The trail notes warn that when heavy rain and high tide coincide, the rivers can be thigh deep. Low tide is at 9:30 A.M. and high tide is at 3 P.M., so as long as we could complete the six-mile road walk quickly enough to hit the beach around low tide and finish before high tide, we would be safe.

Marilyne's habit of rising with the sun put her on the trail by 7 A.M. We are not far behind at 8 A.M. Matteo, however, burned the midnight oil with Paul and is still sleeping when we stop by. Paul offers to cook us brekkie, but we unenthusiastically say no to the bacon.

On the beach, we keep vigilant looking for fairy terns, an indigenous shore bird. There are only ten breeding pairs, with Pakiri Beach being a regular breeding site. We walk softly around the roped off nesting areas, hearing their "tiet tiet" vocal defense calls before seeing their pale grey upper body and white underbody blending well with the sand.

Sandbars make for an easy crossing of our first beach stream, but the real story is in the wind, which is howling continuously like a sad song into our faces. At the second crossing, the water is deeper and wider, forcing us to remove our boots and socks to avoid soaking feet for the rest of the day. As we exit the stream, the low-level blizzard whips up the dry top layer of the quartz sand, hitting us and our now-wet feet like shots of a rapid-fire rifle.

"Well, shit. This sucks," Justin complains out loud. We do our best to dry our feet with our pack towel and hurry to cover them, but the sand is literally pelting us like hail, sending a sensation of pins and needles on every exposed section of skin.

At the end of our coastal walk comes the third and worst stream. It is the widest and looks innocent, but the silty water camouflages the depth. At 2 P.M., we are getting dangerously close to high tide. As icing on the cake, it begins to rain.

Justin enters the stream first and it is up to his thighs. He drops his pack on the other side and comes back in to help me, as I balance my pack above my head.

Wiped from the day, we contemplate staying at the holiday park on the other side of the stream, but it cost $15 per person to camp, and it is just an additional three or four miles into Omaha Forest to freedom camp. We eat a late lunch and I turn on my phone to find a text from Marilyne saying she is camped at kilometer 482.5. We text back to say we will join her.

The uphill to reach the forest is wet and slippery and we find a sheltered spot out of the wind at kilometer 481.5 at 5 P.M., so give up on catching up with Marilyne. As for Matteo, we receive a text a few hours later with his epic tale. Due to his delayed start and brekkie with Paul, Matteo said the last stream was impassable. He tried, but it was up to his neck not even at the halfway mark. Luckily, there was a Department of Conservation worker who drove him the six miles around the stream and he is camped at the holiday park.

The unpleasant weather lingers through the night and we are grateful we found a somewhat protected camp spot, though the tent walls snap like a drum-tight sail in the gusts of wind. I strain to peer out my tent door through the deluge, but watch solid sheets of water descend through the trees.

The thru hiker motif of "why am I doing this?" creeps into my mind again. I push it to the back and begin putting on my hiking clothes—still wet from yesterday—to venture into the madness.

We move through an area of harvested pines, but then the regenerating forest thickens with wet gorse bush mixed with mud. It is difficult to keep my footing on the steep and muddy trail as the forest floor is completely covered by slippery protruding roots. My fall count reaches four. At the Waiwhui Stream crossing, we don't bother to take off our boots in an effort to clean off some of the mud covering our rain pants.

We try to make our way up to the summit, The Dome,

but instead, the trail keeps going down. We stop to turn on our phone to check our location on the iHikeGPS NZ app, showing we are very close to the summit, but not quite there yet.

"Why the hell are we going down then?" I grunt.

We receive a text from Marilyne. She ate dinner at the Top of the Dome Café and is about to leave, cautioning us that the café closes at 5 P.M. It is 4:45 P.M. We should be in a celebratory mood as we are about to hit five hundred kilometers completed, but the possibility of getting to a closed café is a watermark on our excitement.

The trail changes in the last half mile to a well-maintained staircase lined with informative signs about the trees. I can't even enjoy it because we are sprinting.

At 5:01 P.M., we arrive at the Dome Café.

"Your mate told us to wait for you," the friendly server squawks. "What can I get you?"

Another text from Marilyne comes through while we are scarfing down some treats. The next section is closed for logging during daylight hours, which is why we planned to hike through this evening. However, Marilyne warns in her text that there are no good spots to camp, although luckily, she knocked on some doors and found someone willing to let her camp on their lawn.

We debate our move, just as Bill, the café owner, is closing up. He offers to let us camp in the bush on the café property for the evening.

"What about the logging area? Can we walk through in the morning?" I inquire.

"I wouldn't suggest it. They'd be heving a rottie if you did," Bill advises. "And I wouldn't walk the roads. Too dicey. I can drive you around the logging section in the morning."

We make arrangements with Bill to hitch that ride and ask for permission for Matteo to camp with us, should he catch up. We leave a note out directing Matteo to our camp spot.

In the tent, we seriously question our intentions on this trail. We are a goals-oriented couple. We once watched all of the eighty-plus Academy Award Best Picture winners because we could. We want to explore all the National Parks. We want to climb all the state high peaks. We want to thru hike all the trails. Our friends and family have come to expect us to have rad adventures, but it is also okay to try something and fail. We always say 'let's do it' until it's no longer fun, and well, this can't be fun. But, we're in New Zealand. The rules are different. Pigheaded as it may sound, we came all the way over here with a purpose. Forgoing this goal would crush our egos.

Matteo's voice snakes through our tent walls, breaking our discussion.

"Yous guys. This fuckin' trail."

We come out of the tent to exchange combat stories, but the sandflies descend upon our unprotected flesh for their nightly feast of our warm blood. Instead, we carry our conversation tent to tent. Matteo says he plans to walk through the closed logging section in the morning. He says another tramper ahead of us, Ole, did it without any problems.

We never return to our earlier conversation. Instead, we ebb and flow on our logging road decision like the tide does. Ultimately, we decide the possibility of being squashed by giant rolling logs Donkey Kong style is the wrong strategy.

"Let's not break the logger's rule," I sigh. "Just your

trail purist rule."

| 5 |

Urban Walking
Days 22-34: 216 miles

"Do not walk the highway like I did," a text from Marilyne reads.

After ten sunless days, the daffodil-colored ball peaks through grey comforters in the sky on day twenty-two for us. However, the estuaries and tide-dependent walking in this section become more intricate, forcing us to face more anti-purist moments.

The walking route to Orewa is still incomplete in 2014, so the trail notes suggest either hiring a kayak on an outgoing tide four miles down the Puhoi River or walking State Highway One. Marilyne claims her body is still shaking from nerves from being dangerously close to automobiles for the eight-mile freeway route. Of course, our afternoon arrival to the river coincides with the wrong tide. This trail continues to dare my type A personality to loosen up and go with the flow. We decide it is in our best interest to hitch a ride past the highway.

Immediately, a couple picks us up. The male partner has walked sections of Te Araroa and tells us he lives on the South Island in Invercargill near the end of the trail.

"When you get down to Invercargill, look me up and give me a shout," Mike urges as we exit his car at Wenderholm Regional Park, where we plan to camp. I scribble his name down in my journal as he dashes off. We update Marilyne on our location and plans, but she convinces us to hitch a little further to the town of Orewa to catch up to her.

The trail notes describe the beach route into Orewa as a "low-tide rock hop." Considering it is still high tide, we decide against that. Neither of us wanted to hitch again, so we opt to walk two to three miles on the road into town, thinking it won't be as busy as the highway we just drove.

With no shoulder, this couldn't be further from the truth. We keep our heads down and hug the cliff wall bordering the road as cars scrape by us in a few near misses.

Finally, we come upon the sidewalks in Orewa and settle in for the night at Pillows Hostel with Marilyne. It's a good chance to catch up, as we know Marilyne has a few errands to run in anticipation for her planned detour from the trail to meet her husband in Auckland for his holiday next week. The three of us secure a private room at the hostel, then enjoy McDonald's for dinner. We hear from Matteo, who is stealth camping in Puhoi for the night. Starting tomorrow, the group will officially be split up for awhile.

After several nightmares about being run over, Friday dawns with more sunshine, and even though we could have perfect timing for the low-tide zenith, our confidence in the route is paltry. The Okura Estuary can only be crossed at absolute low tide at a specific pole marker in the water and is expected to be hip deep even at that time. In fact, our trail notes state that the Auckland Council does not recommend this route, affirming that Te Araroa is really just an arbitrary line traversing the country. We make our way to the Okura River, where we can also pick up an alternative bush track. We pass lots of boats moored up at the local yachting club, and I feel bold enough that I would ask for a lift across, but we see no one.

At the river, all I observe is danger. Last night was a full moon, making the tides higher than normal. Despite showing up at exactly low tide, the body of water still looks too large and impassable.

"Why even bother trying it?" Justin chuckles. We both shrug our shoulders, resigned to the fact that the trail rules our decision-making. Just a few miles on the Okura Bush Track will take us to the road where we can hitch and meet back up with Te Araroa.

Once on pavement, we find a ride immediately. We tell our driver, Brian, to drop us at Longs Bay Regional Park, where our trail notes say we could camp. Clocking eighteen miles for the day was enough and now that we are in metropolitan Auckland, camping spots are very limited.

It is a madhouse at Longs Bay. Schoolchildren have started their holiday break and I've never seen more people in one place in New Zealand. We locate the ranger station, but receive bad news.

"Thare's no camping in Longs Bay," he frowns. "Hasn't been for years." Justin shows him our map and trail notes, using his persistence to try and change his mind. I can tell the ranger is very busy and has no answers for us, but I let Justin try. Eventually, he surrenders his hopes of convincing him.

We step out of his office to devise a new game plan. It is eight miles to Takapuna Beach Holiday Park. I lean on my poles, asking my body if I have the strength to make it there. A hitch would be smooth with all these people around, although I know where Justin's purist heart lies.

"How do you feel about walking there?" I ask.

Justin lets out an audible sigh. "Let's do this."

We chew the miles down as we weave effortlessly through the suburbs and bays, picking our way through a labyrinth of curved cul-de-sacs, crowded urban beaches and paths behind massive houses with well-manicured lawns. Our map and trail notes need not be taken out at all. Along the clifftop urban footpaths, summer barbecues waft through the air as we become connoisseurs of the fantasy house-shopping scene. It's no matter that we look the part of homeless vagabonds in the affluent section of town. The mansions are noticeably lacking Christmas lights or decorations; I only spy a few trees in the big picture windows.

In our last mile, dusk sets in as we walk along thin sea walls, with the wild sea to our left and grooved sandstone cliff faces to our right.

At 8 P.M., we arrive at the Holiday Park, which is brimming with campervans, no doubt a result of the Christmas holiday five days away. The manager tells us it will be $42 for both of us to camp. Justin implores him to cut us a deal, promising that we aren't even taking showers and will be out by 7 A.M. Unfortunately, we find no holiday spirit and pay the most we've ever paid to camp on a small patch of grass.

As promised, we are up and out by 7 A.M., with only five miles to walk to Devonport Wharf to catch our ferry across to Auckland.

Upon our arrival at the Brown Kiwi Hostel—where we stayed twenty-eight days ago when we flew into Auckland—Hannes, the incredibly helpful and hard-working German hostel manager, grimaces.

"You luuk haggard," Hannes says to us compassionately. "You need food. And a shower."

New Zealand has a population of less than five million people, but one million live in Auckland. The city is a sprawling place sitting astride a grassed over, dormant volcanic field laced by motorways, and whose downtown is a cluster of tall buildings on the harbor, making for an attractive setting. However, the increase in people makes us feel like we are in any big American city. We spend our second zero day of the trek at the Brown Kiwi, eating, watching American football at an American pizza place, catching up on blogging and FaceTiming our families.

Reaching Auckland means twenty percent of the trail is complete and our bodies are feeling that twenty percent. However, the physical aspect is only part of the battle. It's the mental part that brings the strongest down. Most long trails only have a twenty to thirty percent completion rate. The year we hiked southbound on the Appalachian Trail, we were two of the fifty people who completed, out of the 256 who attempted.

Justin and I are a very goals-oriented couple. We like to challenge ourselves. We always say we would rather live our dreams and maneuver our way through the obstacles, even with the possibility of never making it. And so, I try not to dwell on the fact that we've only conquered twenty percent. I know I can at least go another twenty percent.

Despite the maze of concrete prevalent while leaving Auckland, things fall together for me. The blisters on my feet callous over and I start to really grow my trail legs. The rhythm of wake, hike, eat and sleep becomes second nature and I know I am exactly where I want to be.

The days leading up to Christmas include another 40 miles of urban exploration through the suburbs of Auckland, presenting a few challenges. Navigating the confusing city streets and stop lights, listening to a constant spew of humming cars and having to find a place to sleep in the civic setting becomes a regular routine. We try to put ourselves in the Christmas spirit despite the lack of decorations. Given the warm summer temperatures and the fact that we both grew up in snowy environments, it is a familiar holiday in an unfamiliar hemisphere. We belt out Christmas songs and cherish the benefits of road walking—access to cafes, meeting more locals, a quick pace and spotting the creative mailboxes.

But we also take notice of an irritating Te Araroa trend. Now that we have abundant sun, we are able to use our solar charger to juice up our Garmin GPS watch everyday so we track our daily mileage. Well, much to our chagrin, the distance we walk according to our watch does not match the miles laid out on the map or in the trail notes. We are walking more. In Auckland, I read an article about the growing popularity of Te Araroa, marketed as New Zealand's three-thousand-kilometer pathway. However, the article references that the trail is 3,219 kilometers, which would make a lot more sense. I am not happy about this revelation.

Eventually, the vehicular noise gives way to the swoosh of jet engine power as we walk below the flight path for planes to land at Auckland Airport. It feels and sounds like there is a simultaneous tornado and earthquake all day long.

On Christmas Eve, we walk into the Hunua Ranges, first passing The Hotel Clevedon. Our Te Araroa veteran friends suggested we stay here, boasting of its delicious food and comfortable accommodations. Tempting, but, it is only 3 P.M. and I have my hopes set on camping at Hunua Falls, as suggested in the extremely descriptive blog written by a single Kiwi lady, Kirstine, who is currently on the trail in front of us.

Still, we could get a snack at the pub in The Hotel Clevedon; afterall, it is Christmas Eve and that calls for a treat.

As we are finishing up our last strip of calamari, I realize I left our Verizon SIM card at the Vodafone store in Auckland. I had stopped in to check about the process to purchase a second SIM card once our two-month plan ends.

"Are you kidding me?" Justin chides with a dagger of passive aggressiveness. "Didn't you double check before leaving?" In order to derail his typical reprimand, I step away and tell him I will handle it. Yes, I realize it's my fault and my common forgetfulness habit, but I also wish he would give me credit for shouldering all the little details. Did it ever occur to him that I am more forgetful because I have more to think about? Justin canceled his cell phone before we left for New Zealand, so now we share one, and its management falls into my lap of duties.

It is 4 P.M. on Christmas Eve. Any store in the United States would be full of consumeristic chaos at this time, but I still try to call the Vodafone store.

A chipper gal puts me on hold after hearing my woes and comes back to report finding my SIM card and would be happy to pop it in the mail if I give her an address. Unbelievable, but I tell her I am eternally grateful and give her an address down the trail.

Off the roads and into the Hunua Ranges, we travel the five-minute detour to Hunua Falls. This is a more than suitable place to celebrate Christmas Eve and wake up on Christmas so it doesn't just feel like another day on the trail. This is not the first Christmas we've spent away from family, but we've always been stateside and split time with both families. Over the years, we had been waking up Christmas morning at my sister's house in Connecticut as her son and daughter were growing up. One of Justin's sisters just started her own family, so we planned to switch gears and spend Christmas morning with those nephews to watch them grow similarly.

"I cannot believe you are abandoning us," our nine-year-old niece wailed dramatically when we broke the news months ago.

"We'll still send gifts," I promised her.

We are careful to keep low key and delay setting up camp while the Hunua Falls day visitors spill in and out. Besides, hanging out along the rocks and listening as the roar of the falls plays its background music is a superb alternative to baking in our nylon greenhouse. The temperatures have not dropped below eighty-five degrees in a few days.

Christmas morning, I open my tent door and see

something shiny.

"Santa came!" I exclaim, counting a full $1.50 in change. Justin swears he didn't place it there, so I stash it away as an unexpected gift from the falls.

Our Christmas day plans involve twenty miles of walking, mostly in forests. I am, once again, following Kirstine's route laid out in her blog. She cranks some big miles, but always seems to find the best campsites. The Mangatawhiri Swingbridge is situated on the river at the end of a forest section and before a farm section. It seems like the perfect place to celebrate Christmas.

We come upon a sign at the beginning of the Mangatawhiri Forest:

WARNING: THE TE ARAROA WALKWAY IS A REMOTE
TRACK. ENSURE YOU ARE ADEQUATELY PREPARED
WITH WATER, COMMUNICATIONS AND A MAP.

I'm thinking this sign may be four hundred miles too late.

In the forest, an art gallery of ferns lines our trail. There are more than sixty species of ferns in New Zealand's forests, giving a distinction of the tropics. Some grow as tall as sixty feet, like the black tree fern, while others remain short and tickle my legs, like the silver ferns. I am most enamored by the baby ferns, or fiddleheads. Their oversized lollipop is the perfect visual for the unfolding of a fern's life.

I don't think I appreciated the massing of ferns of the Northland forests, probably because I was too busy negotiating the mud and the sheer density of vegetation. The more Kiwis we talk to, the more we learn that they laugh at the well-formed trails in America. That's not the bush to them. At the very moment I am thinking this, my right foot stays lodged between two roots as I am stepping forward across a large puddle of mud. My right foot placement is not strong enough to bring my left foot back, so I remain straddled.

"Babe," I hoarsely sputter out as I realize Justin is not directly clipping at my heels as he usually is. "I need help."

From far away, I hear him bellow back, "Heeeellllllooo. I am coming to your rescue!"

It is not the moment to make me laugh, but it does, so much that a puddle of pee makes its way down my leg.

When he catches up to me, he immediately notices my wet pants.

"Did you just pee your pants?" he mocks.

"Just help me damnit. My foot is stuck."

"This is my favorite Christmas ever. It is the Christmas you peed your pants!"

Eleven hours after we started, we reach the beautiful respite at the swingbridge, cook up our Christmas dehydrated feast of roast lamb and vegetables and enjoy the cotton candy sunset.

Kiwis celebrate Boxing Day, so we wake on December 26 still in the holiday spirit, also knowing that we will go through the motorway stopover in Mercer, which includes a small store, a pub and a McDonalds. We make quick work of the morning miles and arrive at the Golden Arches at 1:30 P.M. On trail is the only time we willingly eat McDonalds.

As we are feasting on our $20 meal—which consists of two burgers, twelve chicken nuggets, two large fries and two sodas—people look on in horror at the quantity and speed in which we are inhaling our food. Generally speaking about Kiwis, meal portion sizes are smaller than they are in America. Further, there aren't many all-you-can-eat buffets or self-serve drink stations, which says a lot about the American diet, but is hurtful to hiker hunger.

We take advantage of free and unlimited WiFi at McyD's, completing our celebration with calls to both families, who are in the midst of December 25th celebrations.

"I still can't believe you abandoned us," our niece repeats.

Following the holidays, we meander along the Waikato and Waipu Rivers. Our trail notes introduce us to another beloved Kiwi term—stopbanks, which are embankments built to prevent flooding of the rivers. The tall grass, wet with dew, sends Justin into a sneezing frenzy. His sneezes match the number of deep cow hoof prints in the hardened mud and the electric fences we cross along these small hills separating the individual farms. After fifteen miles of stopbanks, we hope we would never have to walk along one for the rest of our lives.

The everyday heat reminds us it is truly summer. Sweat trickles down my temples in tiny rivulets, steaming up my sunglasses. It is no surprise that I am constantly thirsty, having sucked down three liters already today. Even Justin, who typically possesses a supernatural ability to drink very little water when working out, complains of thirst. After a Maori woman tells us, "please don't drink from that river," we stop filling up from the Waikato. The murky river, which is approximately 260 miles long, is New Zealand's longest, but has a bad reputation for waste quality. Given the surrounding fertile plains are one of the country's premier dairying areas, we heed the advice and fill up another three liters each at her house, which disappear instantly by late afternoon.

Along the stopbanks lining the farmed lowlands around dusk, a water tank comes into view. It seems like a better choice than the river at this point and we need water for dinner and the next day, so we turn on the faucet and watch as clear water comes out. We filter and fill up. Eagerly, I take a sip. Even with our trusty Sawyer filter, the liquid tastes like cement, but after a full six hours without water in the hot sun, I will drink cement. I flavor it with lemonade power and sip it like it's whiskey.

We make camp under a cabbage tree for shade and as night falls, the possums have races up and down the tree, keeping us awake and still thirsty.

The next day, the riparian path takes us back out to a main road, where we will go through Huntly Golf Course. The trail notes state that the clubhouse is open for food and drink on weekends, noting that walkers are welcome. Timed perfectly to be passing through on a Saturday, we both daydream about cold drinks.

The first thing we notice is the lack of golfers on the well-trimmed golf course for a sunny Saturday afternoon. At the clubhouse, the cafe looks as if it hasn't been open for years. Around back, the men's bathroom door is propped open.

"Well, I might as well christen their throne," Justin says, ducking inside. One of the biggest Crohn's disease markers is frequent and unpredictable bowel movements. On the Appalachian Trail, we kept track of how many times Justin dug a hole for his poop for our blog. We all laugh, but for Justin, flushing toilets and toilet paper is sometimes just as good as a cold drink. I take advantage of the outdoor spigot and drink two liters of water. My thermometer reads ninety degrees as Justin emerges with good news.

"There's a shower in there! I think I'm going to cool off."

"Hell yeah! I'll take one after you! I love Huntly Golf Club!" While Justin is showering, I send a text to Marilyne and Matteo—who are both still behind us, but not together—with information about our recent camp spots and to make sure they stop for a shower at the golf club (they do!).

The place remains empty as we pack up our stuff and move on down the road, refreshed from water and showers. The chimneys of the Huntly Power Station, New Zealand's largest thermal power plant, stand tall in the distance.

We pop into Huntly for a quick resupply at the Countdown grocery store, then head into the Hakarimata Reserve, mimicking another campsite from Kirstine's blog with a beautiful view overlooking where we'd come from. Sunset paints the kaleidoscope of pastels across the sky and we fall asleep to the sound of the nocturnal performances of the possums.

On Sunday, our map tells us we have all road walking. Sunday is the day I recite prayers if I remember. We were both born and raised Catholic and then married in the Catholic Church. We are not very regular in our attendance for mass, but prayer has always been something powerful for me and I find the wilderness to be the best church around. Today's road walk is on sidewalks, making for the best prayer service time because I can zone out, as opposed to navigating with the GPS every fifteen minutes in the forest.

"Hail Mary, full of grace, the Lord is with thee," I chant under my breath. I offer the first one to my mom; she is always the first. Then one for my dad, sometimes two if he is in a particularly ill state. Then my sister, my niece, my nephew, my brother-in-law. Then I move onto Justin's immediate family. Next up, I go through our extended families. Today, I have enough time to get through some friends, too. Of course, anyone I know who is struggling physically or mentally gets bumped up the list. I include a prayer for all the hikers out there on trail.

My eyes drift to the surrounding panorama in between my litany. This is the flattest part of New Zealand we've seen. Every mile or so, there is a dilapidated house plopped on a patch of scorched Earth. Brown grass grows up around the abandoned vehicles and broken toys. I had read that after the Crown confiscated this land from the Maori in the 1860s, they cleared the lowland forest all the way to the riverbanks. A lack of McDonald's bags littering the streets tells me we are still far from Hamilton, an inland city of seven thousand people and our next resupply destination.

A billboard fifty yards away catches my eye. We've hardly seen any billboards in New Zealand. This one boasts of a café, open seven days a week. I turn around and motion to Justin, who pulls out his ear buds.

"If it's anything like the Huntly Golf Club, we're out of luck," he chides.

It is just about noon. I fantasize about the café menu and conclude a meat pie sounds better than the crackers and peanut butter tucked in my pack.

No cars are parked in the unkempt yard surrounding the small building, but a sign almost as large as the structure itself reads:

OPEN 7 DAYS A WEEK

We jiggle the handles of every door, losing a little bit of hope at each locked entrance. The last door we try is unhinged. It opens to the bathroom. Once again, we take advantage of the flushing toilets.

Our afternoon perks up from the desperado landscape and onto a joint walkway/cycleway along the Waikato River that will take us seven miles into Hamilton. Knowing there are several hostel options, we did not make a booking, but look forward to our indoor accommodations for the night.

Weekend warriors share the urban pathway with us, giving their obligatory bewildered looks at our huge backpacks and trekking poles. A few make polite conversation. No one is aware of the trail we are doing.

A family of three sitting on a nearby bench catches our attention.

"Hey, whot are you two doing?" the woman calls.

"Walking from Cape Reinga to Bluff," Justin proudly answers.

"No yar not!" Her eyes practically pop out of their sockets. She stands up and comes closer to us. "Are you mad?"

We lean on our trekking poles thinking this will go beyond the "good on yis" we typically receive from passerbys.

"Where do yis stay?" she continues.

"Well, we are carrying a tent and typically camp," Justin explains. "But tonight, we know there are hostels in Hamilton, so we plan to stay at one of those."

"Oh no yar not," she proclaims. "Yar coming home

with us." She hurries on, turning toward her husband and baby. "I'm Paula, this is Michael and our one-year old, Nathan."

We heard about this supersized level of Kiwi hospitality. Our American friends, Clara and BJ, who thru hiked Te Araroa in 2013, told us locals will open their doors unconditionally and though we live in a world of hypersensitivity to strangers, we shouldn't be suspicious and instead embrace it.

The Salisbury family takes us home and offers up the amenities, including laundry. We occupy little Nathan like he was our own nephew while Paula cooks up dinner for all of us. Dinner conversation comes naturally as we learn about their backgrounds and likewise.

"Whot other activities would you like to do while in New Zealand?" Paula asks over dessert of their garden fruits.

We draft our tentative list, not really thinking much about being tourists thus far.

"Hobbiton is straight away from Homilton, a quick bus ride. You should go!" Paula declares.

"Huh," I nod my head. It was on our bucket list of New Zealand sites to see, but we've been so focused on the trail, we haven't planned any side trips. "We hadn't thought of that."

We hop on the Internet to see if there are tickets for one of New Zealand's renowned tourist attractions, but it is booked solid. Hobbiton, or Matamata, is one of the famed movie sets for *Lord of the Rings* and *The Hobbit*. Oh well, maybe another time.

We wake the next morning refreshed to the smell of eggs, coffee and bacon.

"I called Hobbiton and they hev openings for today! The website wasn't updated!" Paula exclaims assuredly. "I'm free today and would fancy taking yis there, then yis can take the bus back!"

And so, we make a booking for our Hobbiton tour and Paula unselfishly takes two hours out of her day to drop us off for the tour.

In 1998, Peter Jackson hand-picked the Alexander family sheep farm as a movie set for the *Lord of the Rings* trilogy, building thirty-nine hobbit holes and agreeing to dismantle them upon the film's completion. However, bad weather delayed the disassembly and the farmers started scratching their heads when people asked to tour the set. Eventually it was torn down, but when Jackson approached the family again for *The Hobbit*, the farmer worked a deal where the set would be built of sustainable materials for future tours. In the height of the season, the Alexanders now see three thousand people in one day.

Our side trip is immensely enjoyable, reminding us that this is a vacation as well as a thru hike. We return to Hamilton and the trail via bus in the late afternoon. We hope to still tick off some miles into the evening to reach a pre-arranged meeting spot with a trail angel the following day.

During our stateside planning process, a friend put us in touch with Mike and his father, Terry, who lives about forty minutes from the trail south of Hamilton. We sent a package to Terry's house and the idea was they would pick us up for a night off the trail. Of course, this was before meeting the Salisbury family. So even though we do not feel we need another break, we have no intention on missing out on more interaction with the locals.

After the bus drops us off at 5 P.M. in Hamilton, we assess our situation and realize we miscalculated our mileage. Instead of the six miles we thought we needed to cover, ahead lies twelve miles. We travel only nine miles before running out of daylight, leaving us with a higher-than-anticipated fourteen miles the following day to meet Mike and his family. We call Mike and plan a hopeful 1 P.M. pickup.

Beep beep beep. My alarm sounds and I rummage in the mesh pocket of our tent, feeling my watch, phone, Buff and headlamp. It is only 6:30 A.M., but we want to make sure we have plenty of time to squash the fourteen miles. The first six miles fly by, but our luck changes after that.

Our trail notes say to look for an entrance into the Kapamahunga Range "well past the quarry." There are two quarries on the map. After we travel "well past" the first quarry, we see a metal gate with a handwritten note confirming it to be the entrance to Te Araroa. We turn on iHikeGPS NZ to confirm and it seems to make sense.

At first, it appears dismal. We are crossing a minefield of cow patties with only a semblance of a trail. Fifteen minutes later, we spot an orange marker, enough assurance to press on. However, after about a mile, we come to a road with a green Department of Conservation sign indicating the start of the Kapamahunga Track. We had been following the orange markers backwards, sending us in a big circle to the same road we'd just come from!

I lose a battle fighting back tears.

"Why are you crying?" Justin spits. Although I know I might be "ovary-acting," his lack of empathy does not help. My PMS holds its malicious grip as I yearn for more control over this trail, a campaign I know I am losing. However, I need to grieve that loss on my own time, and for now, my tantrum is my antidote.

I let myself cry it out for a few minutes before muttering, "We just," sniff, "wasted time." Sniff. "We are out of water," I take a deep breath. "We have no battery life on the phone to check the GPS. And the sign says we still have four miles on this track and it will take four hours." The estimated times listed on the Department of Conservation signs are absurd; sometimes it takes us two hours longer than the listed time, sometimes two hours shorter. It is already 11 A.M. and I just don't have the gumption to continue.

"What do you want to do?" Justin softens a bit. "I'll do whatever you want to do."

I know Justin is hardcore sometimes and wants to get some miles in after a short day yesterday, but I also recognize my limits.

"Let's walk back down the road and have Mike pick us up there." I feel an immediate sense of relief at that statement.

The Campbells are amazingly hospitable, especially given the fact that two complete strangers are interrupting their family holiday celebrations. Mike and Jan are on vacation from the United States with their two children visiting Mike's father, who lives in Te Awamatu. After about an hour, their kids inquire, "Now who are you?" We explain our very complicated story, how we vaguely know their father through a friend. I can see them processing the information and making a note to self: always pick up random, dirty strangers.

There are Christmas cards and packages full of

unexpected goodies waiting for us from our families. This includes a monocular from Justin's sister and her wife, who are alarmed at how often we lose the trail. More importantly, one package includes a single razor. After thirty-five days and not finding a single razor pack to buy in any New Zealand stores, I am excited to improve my hygiene.

We also take care of another piece of personal business—applying for the Traveling Trainer Team role with Leave No Trace. The application required a video, so having speedy Internet at the Campbells was key for our submission.

During the twenty hours we spend with the Campbells, they spoil us. Mike's father, Terry, and wife, Sam, feed us endlessly. They drive us to the grocery store for a small resupply and we do a bonus load of laundry. Our near-zero day is just the attitude adjustment I need.

| 6 |

A New Year, A New Trail
Days 35-45: 160 miles

On New Year's Eve, our American trail angels, Mike and Jan, drop us at the trailhead for Pirongia Mountain, our first high peak of the trip with an elevation of 3,146 feet. My sixty-liter Gregory Deva backpack has almost reached its load limit of fifty pounds, thanks to the treats from home.

We recognize a fellow Te Araroa walker immediately by his scratched-up legs, major tan lines and ratty shirt. It is Ole, a young German hiker Matteo had told us about.

"De only reason you catch me is because I take four days off in Hamilton," Ole scoffs upon our introduction. "I am very fast. I dink I vill be the youngest person to do de trail." Clearly enjoying the edge he possesses, Ole tells us how he didn't even plan on hiking the trail. It just happened and it comes so easy to him. He also lists endless stories of the trail magic he has encountered. While I play the role of polite listener to Ole's stories, Justin remains conspicuously uninterested.

We start the long upward march on the steep and wet peaty trail. Being out of the cities and back in the muddy forest in the countryside is momentarily comforting.

Soon, Ole—who has the gait of a giraffe and the speed of a gazelle—pulls forward. Now that we are alone, Justin delivers some bad news. One of the dogs at the Campbell's house bit the air valve off his Therm-a-Rest NeoAir X-Lite sleeping pad.

"I tried to fix it, but I'm not sure how it will hold up."

"Oh man. You didn't say anything back at the house. I was wondering what was taking you so long to get ready to go."

"Yeah, I guess I shouldn't have left it laying out to dry because one of the dogs thought it was a chew toy. But there was no reason to tell them and make them feel bad, cause it obviously wasn't their fault."

I'm pondering what shocks me more—that we are down a sleeping pad or that Justin is so upbeat. Most people would describe my husband as even-keeled, but those closest to him know he can often blow a fuse over the smallest details—waiting in a long grocery line or the spinning beach ball on a computer screen. Having a mishap forcing him to sleep on the cold, hard ground would generally fall into this category, but he keeps his cool.

"I'm pretty certain I can fix it," he pipes up. Justin thrives on repairing things and has a knack for improvising. One time, while we were managing a bed and breakfast in the middle of nowhere in Oregon, he jimmy-rigged a plumbing issue during our dinner service. The fix lasted the next seven days until we could buy the appropriate part in town.

Nearing the summit, where Ole is waiting for us on a bench, I hear Justin grunt behind me. The mud claims one of his trekking poles. He simply retrieves the broken half from the thick mud, sits down on the bench and starts fiddling with it.

I pull out a few dried apricots to snack on and try to offer a little sympathy for his string of bad luck, silently wondering if there will be a third misfortune.

"I do not even use poles," Ole sneers. I smile awkwardly and think this comment will send Justin's kettle to its boiling point. Instead, Justin has calmly given up on fixing his pole and attaches it to his backpack.

Proving to have its own microclimate, the weather turns rank at the top of Pirongia, clouding any views and spitting rain.

"Ready?" Justin asks while shimmying his pack back on.

A few minutes later, we pop in the old, well-equipped Pahautea Hut, but just for a preview and to sign into the Department of Conservation Intentions Book. With only five miles completed for the day, there is no way Justin wants to end early, especially after our two previous shortened days. Across from us, there is a brand-new Pahautea Hut still locked until its grand opening in a few weeks. New Zealand has nine hundred Department of Conservation huts and luckily for us, Te Araroa crosses several of them, but mainly on the South Island.

We push down the other side of the mountain, which is more treacherous and slipperier than the ascent. In a semi-controlled glissade through the calf-deep mud, I find it hard to tell where the mud ends and my foot begins. I use my poles for leverage, but they practically disappear in the bogs. Justin is somehow managing the same pace as me with only one pole. It takes us four hours to go three miles to the car park at the bottom.

Ole, Justin and I set up camp off the side of the road. I praise God we have cell service and shoot off e-mails to our contacts at Therm-a-Rest and Big Agnes to request product replacements. Justin successfully jams the broken pole pieces together using a tent pole splint. A proud smile splays across his face and he pulls out tenacious tape to try to fix his sleeping pad next.

"This may be a little trickier. The valve is basically chewed off," Justin scratches his beard. "But, it's worth a shot!"

Though Justin's air mattress deflates several times through the night for a poor sleep, the first day of 2015 unfolds with happy news. Our Therm-a-Rest and Big Agnes contacts both respond with plans to ship the merchandise out to Tamauruni, a town we will reach in the subsequent ten days.

We hike on and off with Ole, who tells us he has never gotten lost or confused on the trail. That night, the three of us set up camp at Mangekotukutuku Stream. I tell Ole we are going to eat dinner in our tent because the sandflies are too bothersome and he arrogantly responds that they are not coming near him at all. In the same breath, he offers to switch sleeping pads with me since his is a little bigger and could fit both Justin and I. Though I decline, I silently appreciate that he has more than just an oversized ego.

Justin applies more tenacious tape to his pad,

undeterred by the fact it is a fruitless effort. We make an attempt to share my mattress along with his slow-leaking pad for the night, but neither of us can sleep comfortably. Thankfully, the grass provides a suitable cushion for whoever falls off the pads.

The trail continues straight uphill from our campsite. The incline—I'm guessing a sixty-degree angle—turns out to be so much worse than it looks. We lumber up the hill, grabbing tufts of dried grass and trying not to eat moss in the process. Following a fence line, we grip the rickety wood like a boa constrictor, struggling to avoid the barbed wire, occasional electric fences and the hedges of prickly plants lining the other side of the trail.

We repeat the same pattern going down the other side of the high-country farm hill. By 1 P.M., the trail spits us out at Waitomo Caves.

Waitomo Caves is an extremely popular commercialized underground cave system where you can spot glowworms, or larvae of the fungus gnats that glow in order to mate. While staying with the Campbells, we had booked a boat tour of the caves, as well as an excursion to go blackwater cave rafting. Some people just hiked without doing side trips, but this trip was as much about vacationing as it was about hiking. We also had reserved our hostel for two nights, given the popularity of the area.

We say goodbye to Ole and go to the Waitomo Caves office to see about getting on an earlier tour. There is room on the 2 P.M. tour, giving us just enough time to clean up a bit. We scrounge through our minimalist belongings in our backpacks for our cleanest shirt. I pull out the wet wipes for each of us. We are by no means clean, but better than we arrived.

Following the magic of the glowworm tour, we continue on Te Araroa to the small village of Waitomo and to our hostel. While eating an afternoon snack of a hamburger, complete with toppings of fried egg and beets—a Kiwi tradition—at the town café, two hikers from Israel come up and already know us by name because of meeting Matteo, who is still behind us. Like many others, Nadav and Goni have gained miles by hitchhiking all the road sections. We continue our conversations learning about customs from their country through the night at Juno Hall Backpackers.

After a great night's rest on a mattress for Justin at the hostel, we send Nadav and Goni back on the trail while we get ready to enjoy our third zero day of the trek. Besides the typical town duties of laundry and Internet, we have our third non-trail adventure planned—Blackwater Rafting. This involves getting into wet suits and jumping backwards off a small waterfall into a rubber tube to float down into Ruakaka Cave, once again spotting glowworms along the way. We prefer this tour over the one from yesterday.

Because of my compulsive forgetfulness, Justin will ask me multiple times if I have this or that when we leave a hostel. It is annoying, but admittedly helpful. So, I am shocked when about a mile down the road from the hostel the next morning, I mention how useful our new monocular will be for this next section of farmland, and Justin realizes he left it at Juno Hall Backpackers.

Justin drops his pack and I find the tiniest patch of shade to wait for him.

Thirty minutes later, I see Matteo coming toward me.

"I just see Jus-tine out for his morning jog," he laughs

as we hug. "I get your text this morning, so I move fast to catch you."

When Justin returns with our monocular, we prance along the trail rapidly for the first few miles as we swap trail trauma stories. Matteo has us beat with a very scary encounter with bulls near Mercer.

"I end up in de paddock with fifty young bulls," Matteo narrates. "I manage to jump outside de fence and climb a tree, but de bulls start to break de fence. I had to stay up there for an hour and half. I sing songs to de bulls. They do not go away. I decided de only way to escape was to jump in the stream, which color was terrible, don't know why. In de end, I manage to escape, but my legs were full of scratches. For some reason, I had burger in my backpack and I celebrate with that."

Almost every time we trek through farmland, there are warnings in our trail notes about tiptoeing around young bulls, but thankfully, we've never had a problem like Matteo's.

The last nine miles of our day are through farmland. However, bulls are not the problem this time. We have heard horror stories from other walkers about this section into Te Kuiti and they quickly come to life for us.

We wander aimlessly through the trackless farm pastures. Just for giggles, it seems the path takes us up and over every bump in the landscape. Even with our trail notes, maps, and iHikeGPS NZ app, it is an arduous task to decode the nonsensical direction of the intended trail. Justin is a master of spotting the sparse orange markers among the green rolling hills, earning him the nickname of Legolas from *Lord of the Rings,* thanks to Matteo.

Things worsen as we confront the infamous tunnel of

gorse. This major invasive plant species in New Zealand grows as thick, spiny shrubs, imitating razor wire. Volunteers for Te Araroa Trust recently cleaned up the area, but we still play tug o' war with gorse for the worst half mile of our day. I walk away with a souvenir of one tear in my pants and countless scrapes, stab wounds and splinters all over the rest of my exposed skin.

Once we reach the center of Te Kuiti, it is already 2 P.M. Our destination for the night is only four miles away, but the sun is hot and we are already knackered.

We stop at the grocery store to resupply for the upcoming six-day stretch of trail. We've run out of our dehydrated meals for now, having sent boxed supplies further south on the trail to towns not as equipped with groceries.

I avoid the judgmental stares of fellow patrons as we fill our cart with Whittaker's chocolate, gummy and sour candies, sugary drink mixes, a bag of Pam's Cheesy Alien chips, a bag of Bluebird's Sour Cream and Chives chips, Vanilla Rounds Biscuits (cookies), salami, cheese, spicy ramen and a few packages of just-add-water Thai variety instant meals. Non-backpackers should be rightfully befuddled by what's in our shopping trolley. Truth be told, our real-life eating habits aren't much better. Even though Justin suffers from Crohn's and has to watch his diet, we know we could do better.

Outside the New World grocery store, under a shaded vestibule, the three of us devour a gallon of New Zealand's brand of Tip Top Boysenberry Ripple Ice Cream in hopes it gives us the motivation we need. New Zealand cows deliver top-notch milk and we've been become accustomed to the five-star yogurt, ice cream and milk chocolate products.

The mid-afternoon treat helps, but we still dilly-dally—lingering at every informative sign as we walk the remainder of the trail through Te Kuiti, the sheep-shearing capital of the world.

Arriving less than two hours later, the free campground at Mangaokewa Reserve is a real treat with flushing toilets and running water. Almost immediately, we are offered beer from some Maori locals who drove in for a night of camping.

"Our ancestors are buried up in the limestone bluffs," one Maori man says while drinking his fifth beer in an hour. "It is our land, so take care."

I'm not about to question a man with a shaven head and several tattoos, including on his face. Here is a perfect case of not judging a book by its cover. Though people have warned us about historic hostility from the Maori toward early European settlers, our overall impression of the Maori people is that they are quite giving and hospitable. Manaki is a Maori term for "treat others how you'd like to be treated." We could all learn from the Maori.

Because of the comfort of the grassy site, we don't break camp until 9 A.M. I slept on top of my twenty-degree sleeping bag last night, as I have done most nights since Christmas. Justin has a forty-degree blanket, which is better-suited for these warm North Island temperatures we are experiencing. Even without an inflated sleeping pad, he stays warm. I wonder how the blanket will fare when we reach the mountains on the South Island.

The reserve provides beautiful scenery walking through a gorge with jagged karst on one side and rich forest on the other. However, the path soon turns tricky as it narrows and slants to the point in which the smallest sneeze could send us barreling down the hill to the roaring creek. Sometimes the track follows too closely to the fence line, appropriately covered in barbed wire and spiky kale, or thistle plants. Between that and the minefields provided by farm animal hoofs and turds hidden by long grass, we are surprised none of us plummet to our death. Cows, sheep, and the occasional dead goats become tedious after a few hours and we stop often by the river for breaks in the shade. Matteo pulls out a Sawyer Mini, the same water filter we have.

"You got a water filter!" Justin applauds. Matteo had been drinking straight from the sources without filtering for the first three hundred miles through Auckland. However, up near the start of the trail, he drank from a river that he later found out had a dead horse upstream and we petitioned him to get a filter.

"I dink about what you say about water and iz good choice," he sighs. "Especially with de dead goats and shit. I want to hike, not die."

After exiting the reserve, we have twenty-four miles of gravel roads abound by farms, making camping a challenge and forcing us to knock on some doors to ask about sleeping in their paddocks. With many people not home, our options thin as we walk further. Finally, a farmer answers at a house.

"Sure, you can camp," he says hesitantly. "but I'm moving lamb at 6 A.M., so I'll need you to be up and out by then."

We wake at 5:15 A.M. to the bleating chorus and a horse peeing near our tents. It is our earliest start on the trail, but probably a good idea given the twenty-five-mile day we have planned. Our goal is Bog Inn Hut in the Pureora Forest.

"I'm so excited to have huts and mattresses in the huts," Justin announces. No matter how hard he tried, the pad is hopeless. His pole, on the other hand, is holding up like a champ.

The long road miles allow us to get to know Matteo even better. While Matteo's English is good, he often does a lot of word searching with "how do you say." Since one of my worst habits is finishing other people's sentences, he is the perfect companion for me.

We learn Matteo is a cook back in northern Italy, mostly in small restaurants and sometimes in the high-alpine huts in the Dolomites.

"I want so much to get to de South Island and see the mon-tins and volleys again," he squeals. "I want to cook again. Cous-cous iz not good."

Talking about food while backpacking is usually a bad idea, but in this case, it leads to a plan for Matteo to make his homemade gravy and pasta in Taumarunui, our next town stop.

"I would like to make dis meal. Iz a recipe of love," he promises.

Matteo likes his luxuries, which is why his backpack weighs more than fifty pounds for this six-day stretch, compared with ours weighing between twenty-five and thirty-five pounds. It does not help that he is carrying a three-person tent for just himself. Our food talk turns to gear talk—particularly tents. I pull ahead from the boys as Justin is explaining the weight difference between a single-wall and a double-wall tent. Gear chat is Justin's calling card. Our speaking tour contract with *Backpacker* enhanced our knowledge and fondness for outdoor gear. We segued from the mobile marketing tour into gear testing and writing. One of the reasons Justin and I work so well together on these content projects is because he has a critical mind to figure out how gear works, while I can assemble his thoughts into a fancy and flowing copy.

With our early morning start, we finish the roads by noon. Justin wrongly hypothesizes that there may be a vending machine at the Department of Conservation Pureora Forest Park Headquarters. Still, he asks the worker, who chuckles, "You're in the bush, mate."

We take an hour-long lunch break at the picnic tables and I am feeling spry as we enter Pureora Forest. We are first following the Timberline Trail, a newly constructed dual cycling and walking track following old bulldozer and haul roads. Our re-entry into the podocarp coniferous forest with its extraordinary range of ecosystems is visually arresting and arouses my nose, too, with the earthy, aromatic takeover. The beam of sunlight pierces the canopy of trees lighting up patches of forest floor. Our notes say it will take ten hours to travel the eight miles to the hut, while the trailhead sign says seven hours. I am in disbelief it will take any more than five hours because of the trail's condition. Te Araroa shows its schizophrenic personality with this perfectly blazed and wide path, a dream tread we rarely see in New Zealand. It is the first time Te Araroa resembles the Appalachian Trail. I reminisce about one of our hardest day on the Appalachian Trail, a day in Tennessee where we walked a sixteen-mile section that just kept going up and mirrored a war zone hit by a tornado, hurricane and landslide at the same time. And still, our hardest days on the Appalachian Trail are nothing compared with what we've experienced on New Zealand's long trail.

We come upon a large totara forest section marred by logging where tall, purple lupine blanket the crown of sun-baked pine needles. A gentle climb leads to Mount Pureora's summit at 3,855 feet with views of where we are headed within the following week—the volcanic mountains of the Central Plateau, including visible Mount Ruapehu, whose northern slopes serve as a ski area. We also spot Lake Taupo, a collapsed crater turned into a glassy lake.

By 6 P.M., right at our five-hour prediction, we reach Bog Inn. The fifty-year-old hut—built originally for forest research—has a reputation for rats, as detailed in the Te Araroa blogs I follow and in the Department of Conservation Intentions Book supplied in each hut. With clear skies above, we spend as much time outside at the picnic table as we can before retreating for the night. Normally, Justin would not be keen on sleeping inside the hut given its rodent reputation and such clear weather for camping. However, the alternative of another uncomfortable night on the ground without a pad appeals less. He pops ear plugs in and hopes a giant rat does not try to snuggle.

If the rats ran circles around my head, I have no idea as I wake well rested. The trail continues to be wide, well maintained and well-marked, although a few blow downs make for occasional obstacles.

Though our maps indicate it is only ten miles to the next hut, in true Te Araroa fashion, it ends up being thirteen miles, with the steepest being the last few. Hunched over and heads hanging, we stumble into

Waihaha Hut near dinnertime. We quickly perk up when we realize the shelter is a significant upgrade from the Bog Inn.

Two middle-age locals, Carole and Tony, are already settled in at the hut. We seldom have the company of other trampers, especially Kiwis, so this is definitely a treat. Now that the couple is retired and their children grown, Carole and Tony plan to spend more time tramping, so we share stories about our journey from Cape Reinga to here. Carole and Tony live in Wellington and had seen signs for Te Araroa, but did not know anything about it. I pull out my maps to show them the Wellington route and they are amazed by this discovery of a national trail in their backyard.

As we are cleaning up our dinner, Carole and Tony step out for a private conversation. When they come back into the hut, Carole has a piece of paper with her e-mail on it.

"When you come through Wellington, we would be delighted to host you!" she announces.

We head in separate directions on the trail in the morning, but hope we can take them up on their offer in a few weeks when we reach Wellington.

Ten miles later, we finish Pureora Forest and return to the roads surrounded by private property fences. Small gaps on the sides of the road become our only viable option for sleeping until we spot a ranch house way up on a hill, hidden behind trees. We feel bad invading their privacy, but would feel worse trespassing. The Maori farmer assures us he has many acres and we are free to pick our spot.

We camp near some of the outbuildings, presumably living quarters for some field workers, though empty at the moment.

In the morning, my intestines do their usual morning routine gurgling and I scan the treeless landscape for a place to dig a hole and do my business. With nothing viable, I slam shut my sphincter muscles and run to the structures, checking all doors. I find a bathroom with no door and test that the toilet does flush before relieving myself.

Motivated by trying to beat the heat and the allure of town food, we crush the sixteen miles of pavement into the town of Tamauruni, arriving at 11:45 A.M. First, we stop at the McDonald's to each devour a Big Mac, a cheeseburger, two small fries and two soft drinks. Justin tops it all off with an ice cream, then of course visits the flush toilets twice before leaving.

We arrive at the Tamauruni Holiday Park where Justin's new sleeping pad and poles are waiting for him. Our plan is to spend a full twenty-four hours in Tamauruni, but we have our work cut out for us. Matteo's task is to cook up a pasta dinner with his homemade gravy as a celebration of completing one third of the trail. Justin's task is to do everyone's laundry and send off a few e-mails, including replacing our boots when we arrive in Wellington. My task is to make the arrangements for the paddle section of Te Araroa.

For more than fifty miles, the trail goes down the Whanganui River, requiring the rental of a canoe or kayak. The Whanganui River is one of New Zealand's nine Great Walks, meaning it is a major tourist attraction and reservations can fill quickly. First and foremost, because we are walking on foot, we can't predict our potential reservation dates until we come within a week of the river.

And you have to make reservations not only with the river outfitters, but for the established campsites along the way. The rental companies work with the walkers as best they can, but during high season, you may have to wait a day or two to start your trip.

Second of all, the official Te Araroa route down the river has changed over the years according to availability of drop off and pick up from the canoe rental companies. There are several put in and take out points along the river. During the past few weeks, I had been reading and taking notes on what route other Te Araroa hikers had used. One option skips a portion of the walking trail, another option depends on tides, another option means more days on the river, another option is ridiculously expensive and another option adds nearly fifty miles of road walking. None of the river put-in access points are at a town, so Te Araroa hikers must hitchhike to the canoe company office to drop food supplies for the river passage. The canoe companies all range in price and their own physical location, adding to the equation.

Knowing there are so many components to consider for this section, waves of restlessness had been waking me the past few nights. I am brooding over it, and my cranky energy is palpable. Even my toes are tense. It does not help that Matteo had no clue there was a paddling portion until he met Marilyne and us on the trail and still does not quite understand.

"I will walk de river," he keeps asserting.

Matteo's questions deafen like a record on repeat. I unintentionally give him a lot of incredibly loud silences despite his constant offerings of "thankyouverymuch." It is just a PMS-induced mood swing exacerbated by my Type

A personality, and we all need to ride it out.

I spend the entire afternoon on the phone with four different canoe companies asking the same questions. How much would it be to go from Point A to B? What about from Point A to C? What about from Point B to C? Where are you located and where would we have to drop off our food? Will you book our campsites for us? Do you have availability for January 16, which is my best prediction for when we will arrive at the river launch site?

Justin comes over while I am on hold with one of the companies.

"How's it going?" he mouths.

I stroke my forehead and shake my head no, hoping my body language will give him a clue as to how burdened I feel.

"Have you asked about a walker discount?" he speaks softly.

"I'm trying!" I hiss. He takes it as a clue to get lost. I hear him mumble "I'm just trying to help," under his breath as he storms away.

With all the information gathered, I fill the boys in over our Matteo's delicious home-cooked dinner. I am a tad less frazzled, armed with all the details.

"But how much iz gonna be Pah-treese?" Matteo demands for the fourth time. Even though I agree with him that you can buy a canoe for the lowest, $185 per-person rental rate I find, basing the decision on cost would add a whole level of unnecessary hassle.

"You guyz. Iz not right. No? Iz a joke. This price cannot be right," Matteo whistles.

Justin agrees with me that the three-day paddling portion from Whakahoro to Pipiriki is our best option.

Three days is in fact the cheapest, plus we don't care for spending the five or seven days on the less desirable sections of the river and want to walk as much of the trail as we can. I also suggest going with Blazing Paddles, a family-owned company who offered to pick up our food from the Tamauruni Holiday Park before meeting us several miles down the trail with the canoes, saving us the hassle of hitchhiking off trail to deliver supplies to them. The downside is we will have the extra fifty-mile road walk following the river trip. Justin trusts my judgment on all I've researched and is happy to go along with my suggestion.

Matteo is still contemplating the cost and less than happy about the extra road walk. I excuse myself to start cleaning up from dinner, leaving Justin to deal with Matteo's barrage of questions. By the time I finish the dishes, he decides to just follow our decision.

"Beautiful. Thankyouverymuch." Matteo says.

Now that our blueprint is laid out, I feel much less stressed. In our tent, I apologize to Justin for my gloom and outbreaks, but he tells me he understands and starts rubbing my shoulders. The truth is, he would be willing to take over, but he knows my strength is planning, even though I let it burden me. I might be slowly surrendering my controlling personality to this trail, but I am still in my element when I am breaking down amorphous and overwhelming tasks methodically with clarity, organization and purpose. Justin balances out my natural tendencies by sending me into laughing hysterias when I need it the most. With every squeeze of his hand on my neck, I feel like a new woman.

The three of us spend a full hour the next morning

doing all our food shopping for the canoe portion. After eating only the lightest nutrition that we can carry in our backpacks for the last forty-five days, we relish in the fact that we have two hard-sided barrels as storage for the rations and can pick out heavier and more scrumptious grub. Our $160 bill for the three-day trip includes a one-liter bottle of Fanta soda, a one-liter bottle of boysenberry cider and one package of Hokey Pokey Squiggles cookies. For dinner, we go with boil-in-the-bag meals—which are much bulkier than our dehydrated meals—but probably a little healthier.

When we return to the hostel to pack everything up, Justin has one of his moments and goes off the deep end.

"All of our food is gone from the fridge and shelves!" he wails. We left six days of our regular backpacking provisions—as well as Matteo's leftover pasta meal meant for today's lunch before walking on—with a note including our names and a check out date of January 11 to safeguard it against disposal. Hostel and campground refrigerators easily fill up with rotten, leftover food, so the owners and housekeepers are constantly cleaning it out. Since we were the only holiday park guests the previous day, the owners greatly appreciated our offer to clean out the fridge. Oddly enough, our food was just about the only remaining items in there this morning.

I rush over to the woman sweeping the grounds, but she tells me the owner actually cleared it out, and is gone for the day.

"Where's your phone?" Justin demands of me, his forehead veins pulsing.

I hand over our phone and Justin's hand is shaking as he dials. Matteo and I pace as Justin spews off accusations about our food to the owner on the other end. I'm not sure how this can be resolved—neither diplomacy nor patience comes easy to Justin—but he is relentless in demanding answers.

"What do you mean you took it to feed your pigs?" Justin squeals and tries his passive-aggressive approach. "You mean to tell me you gave your pigs an entire Whittaker's chocolate bar and homemade pasta sauce? Didn't you see the note saying it was ours with tomorrow's date?" I know his bark is worse than his bite, but my distaste for confrontation and mousy, pushover approach would have probably apologized to the guy for his mistake. From our experience working in the busy hospitality industry, I realize these things can be easily overlooked.

The owner decides to come back to the campground in an effort to make things right. He helps us salvage what we can from the trash, which includes our detailed note not to throw anything away. He offers to comp all our stays, but we let him reimburse Matteo only, mainly because of Matteo's hard work over the homemade meal. The Whittaker's chocolate bar, however, remains amiss.

By the time we sort and store all our supplies with big and bold labels for pickup from the paddling company, it is 2:30 P.M. The apex of the day's heat in New Zealand during this time of year is exactly between 3 P.M. and 6 P.M. and with eleven miles of roads ahead of us, we know the mercury will boil.

All three of us lather up on sunscreen before stepping out onto the sizzling black tar. Before I could say melatonin three times, the ultraviolet rays on steroids have done their damage.

"Babe, did you put sunscreen on your face?" Justin

scolds. "You're getting really red!"

"Yes!" I scream, storming ahead, as if my shade of crimson is his fault. Both our tempers are undoubtedly bent out of shape, so we walk apart from each other on the road, silently moping.

Nonexistent clouds turn up the microwave and by 4 P.M., I feel more and more like an ice cube on an oven range. The tar from the pavement is melting into the soles of our shoes and to the tips of our trekking poles as we walk. Excitement billows when I see a truck approaching; it means a fleeting breeze.

We drag our low, overheated mood into the small, desolate town of Owhanga, hoping for the saving grace of a cold drink. Still muted, the three of us simultaneously read a sign in one of the storefront windows:

WELCOME TO OWHANGA TE ARAROA WALKERS. PLEASE CALL AND HAVE A DRINK WITH ME. KAREN

We all exchange high fives knowing the first part of our day is about to be erased.

I whip out my phone and call the number listed. Karen answers and is ecstatic. She says she is hosting a picnic at her organic blueberry farm down the road and will come pick us up.

The cold drink dreams come true with additional treats of barbecued meat, salads and cakes, as well as fresh blueberries. Karen is hosting the get-together for a friend who is newly engaged. I could say we felt out of place, but Karen made us feel like part of her family. She is used to welcoming strangers, as she hosts WWOOFs, young tourists who are "Willing Workers On Organic Farms."

We move from conversation to conversation among the thirty or so people at the party, making sure to stop at the buffet table in between every group. I even meet a fellow female writer, Margie, who used to own the blueberry farm and just published her first memoir. I share with her my dreams of publishing a memoir about our trek across New Zealand and she tells me I must pursue it until it becomes a reality.

Karen does not have to twist our arm when she offers to let us sleep in the yard of her house/bed and breakfast, The Shack. She even insists we cool down with a nice shower. A beautifully clipped lawn allows us to sleep sans rainfly without the threat of dew, exhibiting views of the Milky Way smeared above like butter on toast.

Refreshed by the still unbelievable Kiwi generosity, our next two days we crisscross through the Forty-Two Traverse, a multi-use track on abandoned forest roads. With toi toi frond draping the wide thoroughfare, we stay on our toes around every corner, prepared to jump off the path to avoid the oncoming four wheelers.

Periodic views reveal three monsters looming in the distance. Much of the North Island is volcanic in origin and this upcoming sector will weave us around three active volcanoes, including Mount Ngauruhoe. The mountain's symmetrical cone shape is best known as Mount Doom in *Lord of the Rings*.

| 7 |

Volcanoes and Rivers
Days 46-57: 231.8 miles

Day forty-eight is our best day on the trail so far. It is
the day we complete the Tongariro Alpine Crossing,
another one of New Zealand's nine Great Walks.

The one-day twelve-mile traverse serpentines through
three intermittently active volcanoes: Mount Ruapehu,
Mount Tongariro and Mount Ngauruhoe (also known as
Mount Doom). Mount Ruapehu is the highest peak on the
North Island at 9,177 feet and though active as recent as
the 1990s, the snow-covered volcano has two commercial
ski areas on it.

The most recent and well-known eruption for any of
the three volcanoes was on August 6, 2012, when Mount
Tongariro erupted for the first time in more than one
hundred years. Though no one was injured, flying rocks
damaged Ketetahi Hut, which is situated less than a mile
from the lava-spewing site along the Tongariro Alpine

Crossing. The track did not reopen until 2013 and the hut remains closed to overnight visitors still today, but serves as a day shelter.

We anticipate mobs of people not only because of the recent volcanic action, but because of our mid-January timing, the route's Great Walk status and the fact it is a national park, New Zealand's first actually. About one third of the country is a protected national park and while their parks don't see the crowds America's National Parks see, their Great Walks do.

Tourists march heel to toe in a steady stream on the Great Walks. Since Te Araroa comes from the north and the majority of the day visitors hike north on the Tongariro Alpine Crossing, we will be going against the caterpillar train of roughly seven hundred people, fewer than usual given it is a Monday. To optimize solitude, we plan an early start.

Yesterday, we hiked a mere twelve miles and end up just before the Tongariro carpark and trailhead. We originally thought we'd camp at the holiday park, less than five miles from the trailhead. However, when we arrived at 1 P.M., the staff on duty quickly informed us not only that we could not check in until 3 P.M. to the campground, but we could not fill up our water bottles, nor use the restrooms in the meantime. Shattered by their unfriendly policy, we decided not to camp with them and moved to the building next door to at least sit in the shade for lunch. The sign read "Adventure Headquarters" and through the windows we saw ski equipment.

I walked around back to look for people, and instead discovered a working water hose. Matteo and Justin agreed that desperate times called for desperate measures, and we all filled up completely before moving on down the road to freedom camp just before the trailhead.

It turned out we could not sleep at the Tongariro Crossing trailhead because there were "no camping" signs all over, plus heaps of people around finishing their day hike and shuttle buses coming and going. Instead, we found a tucked away spot off the main road.

Our alarm wakes us at 6 A.M. and it is thirty-nine degrees, but the skies are clear. While I am waiting for the boys to finish their packing, I walk in circles around the parking lot to keep my blood flowing. A shuttle bus driver offers me a tea and I call him a saint.

We commence the exposed walk up the old lava tongue by 7 A.M. We straggle behind Matteo and promise to meet up on the other side of the crossing.

The track standard is a major upgrade from Te Araroa's typical tread, being manicured, well-trodden and with switchbacks making the four-thousand-foot climb easier. At every switchback turn, I pause for the expansive valley views, spotting Lake Rotoaira and Lake Taupo among the fields of green. I finally feel like the trail is rewarding us for our hard work.

Plumes of white smoke are punching into the colbalt sky, seeping sulfurous gas from the nearby smoldering vents. We pass several signs warning us we are in an active volcano zone.

NO STOPPING

MOVE QUICKLY THROUGH

KEEP YOUR STOPS TO A MINIMUM

We pause halfway through the climb at the Ketetahi Hut, sitting at 4,700 feet. There are still big bites taken out of the hut's roof and the rotten egg smell is strongest in this area, with a crater steaming less than a mile away. Inside the hut, I pull my shirt over my nose as the stench worsens and wonder if the hut will ever be open for overnight use again.

Near the top, at six thousand feet, everything becomes electric. Four emerald, opalescent crater lakes tinted by thermal minerals offer bursts of color among a darkened earth. The exodus of people, selfie sticks, iPads and Canons with bazooka lenses begins around 10 A.M. shortly after the lakes, but we cruise our way across the Mars-like caldera landscape. Before descending lower, I take one more look back and it doesn't take much to imagine the eye of Sauron on smoky Mount Doom or a Battle of the Orcs in Mordor.

We reunite with Matteo at Mangatepopo Hut, which sustained no damage from the eruption and still hosts overnight guests. The three of us carry on to the ski village of Whakapapa, stopping to eat a late lunch. I cannot resist an ice cream, overpriced at $10. That night, we stealth camp along the banks of Whakapapita Stream, watching as the sun dips behind the towering Mount Ruapehu, its whipped cream-covered flanks gleaming from the lowlight.

The following day starts with the Fishers Track, a grassy vehicle path abound with fertile land, where we cause unintentional stampedes among wild goats and sheep. The cows, on the other hand, just stare, as if we just walked into a bar and the record scratches to a halt. The bucolic landscape offers a unique juxtaposition of lofty ranges with farm houses in the forefront.

After the nice grass underfoot, thirty miles of mixed paved and gravel roads stand between us and the village of Whakahoro, where we will meet Blazing Paddles to start our river trip on January 16.

Once again, we are forced to seek private land for sleeping, but this road has few homes. The only sign of human life we see is a gentleman driving by us twice on an ATV with a gun and dead animal carcasses piled in the back. We make sure to wave both times we see him.

We reach the end of a fence line and pause at a winding driveway with a scintilla, shambled, white farmhouse about thirty yards away. Since the house is so close, we decide the three of us should walk up together. It is Justin's turn to do the talking though.

There is a gate to reach the front door of the house, but we stand outside it. A man wearing crusty combat boots, tattered blue jean shorts, a faded t-shirt and a misshapen ball cap is sitting on the stoop, his legs spread as wide as the stairs. His lower lip is pursed. His calloused hands tightly grasp a bolt-action hunting rifle with a silencer across his body. I recognize him as the man we spotted earlier on the ATV.

He spits. "Well, I was wondering when you get hare."

My eyes dart in Justin's direction. He shifts his hips and leans on his trekking poles. He cocks his head and furrows his brow, "Oh," he asks casually, "so you were the guy who passed us up on that hill a few times?"

"Sure was."

"We were wondering," Justin stammers, "if we would could get some water?"

"Ya ya ya. No worries mate. I've got that." He spits again.

I try to stand up straight without grimacing and force a smile to show my appreciation.

"We were also wondering," Justin continues bravely, "if we could camp on your paddocks. Maybe out front by the hay bales?"

"Aaah, naw. You don't have to camp thare. You can camp rate hare on my lawn, ay." He gazes up toward the hilltop. "Thing is. I have to go make a phone call up thare on the hilltop. I'll be gone for two hours. Make yourselves at home in thare," he motions behind him to the inside of the house, "or out hare." Then he sings music to my ears, "Reckon you'll want a shower mates?"

Before we can question him on all that good news, he is back on his ATV and off toward the hillsides.

"Did you get his name?" Justin asks me.

"He never said it!" I laugh.

"Beautiful." Matteo chimes in. "Just beautiful."

"Well, I'm going to go take a shower before he comes back and realizes that he just left his house in the hands of three transients." I am particularly excited about this unexpected shower because I smell like a taco truck and I am on my period.

Our stranger friend returns and introduces himself as Ellen, or Alan; we couldn't quite tell through his accent. We get to chatting while he pops open a beer. Ellen works for the Department of Conservation setting possum traps up in the hills we just walked. This is not his home, or farm; he just rents the place for his weekday work schedule. He returns to his real home in Palmerston every weekend. Ellen moves onto his second beer. Splaying his gold tooth glinting in the sun, he says, "I would offer you a bare, but I only have twelve lift."

After his sixth beer and delightful conversation, we all retire for the night—us comfortably set up on his lawn and he inside the house. Short grass again allows us to keep the rainfly packed away.

We wake early to try to beat the sun for our twenty miles of road walking. All of us plug in our music and agree to take a break every two hours. Down below, the Whanganui River slices a deep cleft through the siltstone countryside and I am excited to trade in my trekking poles for paddles tomorrow. The day drags, disrupted only by the sheep herding trucks passing by and leaving us in a smog of dust. One smaller vehicle zooms past us back and forth three times, spraying us with chunks of gravel the size of apples. The events and ninety-degree temperature put my body on slow roast as we stroll into Whakahoro at 3 P.M.

Whakahoro is a bustling village of less than ten structures, including the Blue Duck Café, a popular jumping off point for all the paddlers. The owner is enamored by Te Araroa walkers and offers us a free cold drink upon arrival. Three other Te Araroa soldiers join us from the river. A young Australian couple, Jeremiah and Kelsy, and Florian from Germany started paddling at Tamauruni and will take out at Whanganui, opting for the seven-day trip. We exchange stories until they have to get back on the river to finish their day.

The following morning, Blazing Paddles meets us with our boats, supplies and fresh plums as an extra. Justin and I share a canoe, while Matteo is in a solo kayak. Their three-minute safety briefing instructs us to point our vessels downstream and steer clear of jet boats.

Among several other river enthusiasts, we start paddling at 10:30 A.M. Matteo, having never paddled any river, immediately capsizes. He is not alone. There are all levels of experience on the river, more often those in the beginner category.

For three days, we snake our way down the Whanganui River. The waterway used to be a river boat trade operation through the 1920s before better roads and railways took over. Its layered banks are speckled with fossil shells, interspersed with eruption sediment from the nearby volcanoes. The bush-clad hills are mirrored in the peaceful channel. Countless waterfalls and caves dot the steep-sided gorges.

We cover the fifty-four miles of river with little effort. Even when we aren't paddling, we are still clocking miles faster than we would on foot. A handful of benign rapids bully and release us with an adrenaline rush, but Justin and I handle them all well and never flip.

"How do you guys do it?" An American tourist cries to us. "You look so calm, cool and collected going through the rapids."

Justin has been paddling since he was a teenager and used to be certified by the American Canoe Association as an instructor. I only picked up the sport in my twenties. The truth is, I just let Justin shout commands for me to follow when we are in a canoe. He may say, "paddle left!" but I suddenly become directionally challenged and just jab my oar wherever it is at the whooshing vortex.

More often, we maintain a leisurely pace, making sure to explore and enjoy the scenery. This includes a stop to the Bridge to Nowhere in Whanganui National Park.

In 1936, the New Zealand government erected the bridge with the intention of also building roads when they offered their World War I veterans blocks of farming land in the backcountry for their service. A valley community emerged, but the farming enterprise did not last long due to poor soils and the pioneers abandoned the area by the 1940s, leaving the concrete structure unused in a sea of tree ferns as only a symbol of a doomed experiment. Even though the piece of history is only accessible via boat or foot, it is one of the most visited attractions in the area.

Given the summer crowds on the Great Walk, our designated campsites along the river resemble a music festival rather than riverside oases with tent wall to tent wall setup. Thankfully, the crowds are not a bother. What is a nuisance are the sandbastards, as they should be called. On the chain of evilness, we decide sandflies are at the top. Despite layering up as much as we can every time we stop moving, we suffer the greatest blood loss on this trip thus far as the gnats munch wads out of our skin. Our meal times resemble a ho-down, slapping our calves and arms rhythmically to fight the blood suckers.

On day fifty-three, Blazing Paddles meets us at the river in Pipiriki to swap out the boats for our backpacks—again handing us fresh plums. Back on our feet, we make our way to camp for the night in the village of Jerusalem. A local Maori woman lets Te Araroa walkers camp on her land and sells ice cream, a suitable reward for three days on the river.

"In the end," Matteo surmises, "I would rather to walk than paddle."

We have about fifty miles left leading to Wanganui, one of New Zealand's smallest, oldest and most remote cities, sitting at the mouth of the Whanganui River, where it empties into the Tasman Sea. The government changed the spelling of the river to reflect the Maori "Wh" in 1991, while the city is more often spelled without the "h."

Our plan is to hitchhike the non-Te Araroa road miles to town, while Matteo opts for the human-powered route on the gravel road along the Whanganui River. At the rate of three cars per hour, however, we don't score a ride until fifteen miles down the road when the seventeenth vehicle screeches to a halt to rescue us.

A young Kiwi couple, Richard and Lucy, pick us up. They are on holiday this Monday for Wellington Anniversary Day—the celebration of the arrival of the first organized settlers to New Zealand—and are sightseeing along the river. They ask if we don't mind pulling over a few times along the way and we tell them anything is better than walking.

Richard has his eye on a "flying fox," or a zipline, that goes across the river. We pull off and are examining the rusting zipline, as well as the accompanying cable car contraption on a second line, when another car pulls up.

"Do you wont to try it?" Mark dares. He walks to an electric box and fiddles with some buttons. "I'm going across to grab something from my house."

Richard volunteers to try the flying fox and, without giving it a second thought, grips the rope suspended from the cable and pully, wraps his legs around the tiny seat attached, runs downhill and lets gravity propel him across the river. Meanwhile, the rest of us pile into the tin box, which is not manifesting much more safety. Mark tells us he has owned the property for a long time and both apparatuses were built in the 1950s. One time, when the Whanganui flooded, he used the cable car to bring a couple of cows across.

With our epinephrine mildly activated, the four of us bid farewell to Mark, and Richard and Lucy drop us in

Wanganui. Having arrived after 5 P.M., we ask the Wanganui hostel owner if we can hang around in the courtyard after our 10 A.M. checkout the next day to use the Internet, and he says yes. We are starving, so we decide to hold off on showers and laundry in favor of town food.

After scarfing down roughly four thousand calories—each in the form of salad, bread, fried flounder, fries, cookies and a beer for Justin—we get to work on our hygiene. It has been eleven days since our last laundry cycle and it shows. I return to the hostel front desk to retrieve change for the laundry and he tells me the washers turn off at 6:30 P.M. It is 6:32 P.M.

So, we do as every weary traveler would do. We resort to cleansing our most crucial items—one pair of underwear and one shirt—in the bathroom sink. It wouldn't be suitable for showing up at your nine-to-five employer, but it gets the job done as the dirt, sweat, mud and river water melt from our clothes, turning the water a grayish brown.

We check out of our room well before 10 A.M. and set up shop at one of the property's picnic tables to finish our Internet duties. Using the crawling Internet connection, I start uploading the pictures and text for our blog post, while Justin returns a few e-mails. At 9:55 A.M., Matteo saunters in.

"I hike sixty kilometers yesterday, so had twenty kilometers left this morning. I will take a week off," he declares. Matteo had been telling us about a music festival near Wanganui that was calling his name. It seems the group will be split up once again.

About this time, a different hostel worker, who we hadn't met, comes over.

"When will you two be leaving?" he pries disdainfully in a British accent.

"I don't know, maybe noon or so," I return casually.

"Checkout's at 10 A.M. I've never met lazier walkers than you two!" His condescending tone surprises me.

Justin defends, "We ran it by the guy who checked us in yesterday and he said it would be no problem for us to sit in the picnic area after checkout."

"Well it is a problem," the man huffs. "You don't go to a restaurant and sit at their tables after you've eaten and they've closed!"

Not wanting to fight or cause any more of a scene, we acquiesce grudgingly. We say a rushed goodbye again to Matteo, knowing this is likely the last time we will see him, probably for a long time.

This unpleasant hostel encounter on day fifty-five of our trek leaves a stain on our happiness for most of the day, although it is the only negative interaction of the trip.

The route out of Wanganui follows State Highway Three—until the proposed alternative coastline route is approved. The trail notes read:

SH3 IS AN EXTREMELY BUSY ROAD, SO TAKE
EXTREME CARE

With that warning, we are surprised when we discover a wide shoulder. Still, we spend the afternoon listening to a steady stream of cars, trucks, campervans and motorbikes, all watched over by a blazing sun, leaving us in a giant dust cloud.

Despite my jaded memories of the Tasman Sea from our first few days on Ninety Mile Beach, I am elated to see the windblown coast again. After receiving the unexpected good news they allow Te Araroa walkers to stay for free at the beach campground eighteen miles from Wanganui, we finally relax, watching the sun quiver down into the cobalt ocean like a sunnyside-up egg.

In the morning, I call to make arrangements to stay in Bulls. It seems too good to be true, but our trail notes list a homestay. For $50 per couple, we can stay in a bed, take a shower and do our laundry. This rate is cheaper than any of the seven hostels we've stayed in so far, and even cheaper than some of the campgrounds. I call Jo, the women listed as the contact, to make our reservation. She assures me that tea (what we Americans know as dinner) and brekkie are also included, as well. I am still skeptical.

Our walk begins five miles along the black sand Koitiata Beach. Pieces of driftwood and broken shells are strewn all about. Pale tree trunks and green shrubs protrude from the wind-rippled onyx granules, twinkling underfoot. It is the kind of beach where goths go on holiday, or where one would film a horror flick, maybe called "Satan's Sawmill."

Post-beach, we skirt around another closed logging zone devoid of the sound of chainsaws and lumberjacks. I start to think these segments are merely a cruel joke to make Te Araroa walkers record more time on blacktop.

At 4 P.M., we arrive at Jo's Mayhem Roost, also known as paradise. Not only do we have a bed, but it is in a separate unit from the house with our very own bathroom. I apologize to Jo as I gather our pungent laundry—now thirteen days since its last washing—into her beautiful washer.

Before dinner, their children show us around the family farm. Having an eight-year-old explain about sustainable living makes my heart full.

Jo's partner, Mike, is preparing to slaughter a lamb and asks is we would like to watch. Justin stands in the shadows, watching with one eye closed. As for me, I take photos and don't blink. Though gruesome, I find it humbling to watch what my food endures to make it to my plate.

Jo and Mike lay out a feast of lamb, venison, sausage, potatoes, beans and salad for dinner. Coupled with beer and New Zealand's famed meringue dessert, pavlova, we consider taking a zero day.

Like so many others, Jo and Mike never realized the trail went through their town and right by their house until they noticed people with big backpacks and walking sticks coming through at a fairly steady stream. That's when they decided to open their home to trampers in 2015, thinking it would be a wonderful educational opportunity for their children. Justin and I mark their first, but not their last, visitors. Jo puts up a fight when we hand over the $50, but we insist she take the measly funds, telling her she really actually needed to raise the price.

After a hearty breakfast of eggs, toast, hash browns and bacon, we dutifully drag ourselves back to singing the tar-sealed blues in the blazing heat. We have four days with ribbons of asphalt stretching on and on through the English settler towns of Bulls, Feilding, Bunnythorpe and Palmerston North.

To our surprise, each town brings a treat. Bulls has a widely held sense of humor with all puns intended. The rubbish bins say "Response-A-Bull." The public restrooms say "Relieve-A-Bull." The enjoya-bull signs certainly break the humdrum.

I can tell Justin is most likely hurting, not just from all

the road walking but likely from his Crohn's. His joking disposition has surrendered to knee-jerk reactions, so I keep conversation to a minimum. He'll tell me about his pain when he is ready to.

Jo finds us halfway through our day to bring us two Sprites. I leak tears a little, saying thank you and goodbye to her again. Her gesture is something my mom would do. I ask Justin if we can take a break so I can call my mom. I need to hear her voice to fend off my momentary homesickness.

In Feilding, the big excitement is Kowhai Park. Its aviary houses all the birds we've inevitably heard in the bush, but could never spot, like the kakapo parrot and the flightless takahe.

Also notable are the electronic toilets in Kowhai Park. You enter, press a button to lock the door and a polite voice says you have ten minutes to do your business. The voice then wishes you a nice day when you leave. Kiwi public loos have been as unique as their mailboxes and I love and appreciate their cleanliness and availability. In fact, I bet there could be a whole New Zealand trip dedicated to toilet tourism.

In Bunnythorpe, we grab an ice cream treat at the local dairy and pass the closed-down Glaxo factory. Glaxo is part of the now-famous pharmaceutical giant GlaxoSmithKline. Over the years, I have spent so much time writing about GlaxoSmithKline for my medical writing jobs, so the nerd in me is legitimately excited to see the company's birthplace.

Traveling along the railway line, the trail veers momentarily off the road onto farmland. As we hop over a dozen stiles and a few locked gates in quick succession, we wonder if the Te Araroa signs were placed here by mistake. We reach the small patch of public land designated as a "paper reserve," really our only option for freedom camping unless we want to stay in town.

We set up the tent under the pillars of pine trees with hopes they drown out the nearby train. I tackle most of the camp duties tonight. Justin finally admits his back and legs have been hurting since Wanganui. We attribute the small Crohn's flare up to the influx of town goodies and beer these last few days. I convince him to take something for the pain, and silently hope his body responds with healing.

I dream a train is hurtling down the tracks toward my house. It is close to the truth. The bright side is an early start to the day, thanks to the 6 A.M. train schedule.

| 8 |

Our First Real
Mountain Range
Days 59-63: 79 miles

I can tell Justin's Tylenol P.M. has worked when he sleeps until 8:30 A.M. Although his back and legs still trouble him, we both hope it's not a full-on flare up and that he can just soldier through the pain, then rest during the two zero days planned next week in Wellington. Having Crohn's for his whole adult life means he lives with a broken body. His mantra is no amount of trials, tribulations and setbacks can stop him from pursuing his passions.

We make sure to take lots of breaks on our way to the Makahika Outdoor Pursuits Centre. Based at the foothills of the Taraua Range, the residential leadership camp allows Te Araroa walkers to stay free of charge when they are not busy with programs. I had exchanged e-mails with

Sally, the woman who runs the facility alongside her husband, John. I simply asked about camping. Her response was:

"We have a cottage for you to stay in and join us for a meal. There is no cost; it is our pleasure to host TA walkers."

Once again, we are excited to have some one-on-one time with Kiwis, not to mention this could give Justin a tiny reprieve. When we read the sign at the center's driveway, we know we are in for a treat:

TRAIL WALKERS WELCOME: HOT SHOWER, COLD
BEER, NICE BED

Sally greets us in the driveway with two citrus beers, showing us to our private cottage and instructing us to relax for the rest of the afternoon until dinner at 5:30 P.M. Our private quarters include a queen-sized bed with a view, our own bathroom, kitchen, unlimited Internet and laundry. Since it's only been four days since our last clothes washing, I don't bother doing another load.

Sally and John cook us prawns, pork roast, potatoes, corn on the cob, beetroot, zucchini and rhubarb pie. They are inexplicable trail angels without knowing it. They refuse to accept money, but we stuff their hands with $20 to buy more beer for the hikers behind us, at least. We both secretly wish the weather were foul, giving us an excuse to spend another night at this oasis in the forest, but know we have to take advantage of the calm expected the next few days.

The Tararuas are notorious for two things: erratic atmospheric patterns and hard tramping.

The range's close proximity to the Cook Strait serves as a funnel for the nastiest elements. Between snow in every season, high winds and resulting deaths, Tarauas' adverse weather events have been enough to scare a few hikers into skipping the section altogether. Our weather report predicts two clear days, followed by several days of storms. Though we hope to traverse the exposed part of the range during the two-day window, our bags are packed with five days of food as suggested. If we must, we will hunker down in the huts that provide a beacon of hope in foul conditions.

The other piece of the equation is that Te Araroa's route spans twenty-five miles, gaining ten thousand feet of elevation and losing eleven thousand feet. This constitutes more climbing than we did in the first nine hundred miles of the entire trek.

With fluffy, bunny-tail clouds dotting the bright azure sky on January 26, we head into the Tarauas. Before leaving Makahika, I send off an e-mail to Carole, predicting an arrival of January 30 in Wellington. We arranged to stay three nights with our new friends whom we'd met a few weeks ago at Waihaha Hut in the Pureora Forest. I tell her it will be just us and no Matteo, as he just restarted his hike in Wanganui after his music festival diversion.

Day one in the Taruaras packs its punch with the largest concentration of the elevation gain. We climb through a labyrinth of primeval forest, with gnarly twisted beech trees groaning from the weight of the thick moss and lichen enveloping them. Drooping tree ferns reach out to greet us in this otherworldly existence of a fairytale world.

The single track is tidy and has plentiful markers, unusual for Te Araroa. Being so close to the city of Wellington, the Tarauas are a popular stomping ground for hiking, hence the high level of trail maintenance. I wonder if the whole Te Araroa will ever be fully maintained like our popular long-distance trails in America. On the Appalachian Trail, there is a white blaze every seventy feet thanks to more than five thousand volunteer trail maintainers. With far fewer volunteers for Te Araroa Trust, their efforts are spread thin.

Our goal is the second hut on the Taraua track, Te Matawhai, and after seven hours, we reach it. All the muscles in my body hurt, but Justin collapses like a felled tree, so I leapfrog to the lead on camp duties to let him recuperate. Even though the hut sleeps eighteen, no one else shows up for the night. We down Tylenol P.M. and can barely stay awake past 8 P.M.

Our 7 A.M. wake-up time is in anticipation of an even bigger day. We hope to bypass two huts and make it sixteen miles to Waitewaewae Hut, at the boundary of the Tarauas. Nearly all sixteen miles is exposed on ridges, crossing creased hills covered by alpine tussock. I cringe at the thought of being caught in heinous weather and nod to the blue skies above.

The hills are bumped and humped in an almost cartoonish way, with textured rippling grooves and hypnotically waving grasslands in the winds. For the first time in awhile, we use our thighs for gravity defiance. Although we sweat out half our body weight, the lofty peaks heighten our senses and nourish our souls. Justin's Crohn's pains have dissipated for now, proving the point that motion is lotion, with a little help from pain relievers.

At the highest point of 3,655 feet on Mount Crawford, we pause to soak in the 365-degree views. In the distance, the South Island summits chisel the sky. The reality of being close to the end of the North Island sets in. All day long, we had been enjoying long slow conversations about our life and what's next. Our minds and conversations are mostly on the Leave No Trace job we applied for on December 30 when we were staying with the Campbells. We should be hearing if we made the interview round this week. Because it's a Skype interview, the timing aligns well with the reliable Internet we'll have while staying with Carole and Tony. The job would begin in April, right when we expect to finish the trail and our Visa expires. We often don't plot more than three to four months out, but this year-long life blueprint appears to be falling into place perfectly.

From Mount Crawford, it is just four miles downhill to the hut. For once, I do not feel dead on my feet and am satisfied we will be there in no time.

What we soon realize, though, is that the gradient of this downhill would make an escalator weep. Without switchbacks again, the forest trail is better suited to abseil. We stab the Earth with our trekking poles and tentatively step on untrustworthy solid surfaces—like wet roots—at an impressive one-mile per hour pace. Though we escape unscathed, I end up on my back four times.

Our snail crawl down the impossibly long mountain ends at an impossibly long swingbridge. We've crossed a few swingbridges on the trail so far, but the others seemed more stable. Pendulous in nature, this one is woven together with steel wire, chest-high on the sides. Small rectangular plates of aluminum are spaced every foot or so in case you don't feel comfortable walking on the mesh alone. Perched twenty-five feet above the river, two steel cables secure the bridge to the eroding banks. The sign warns of a one-person load limit. And we have to trek the quarter of a mile across it to reach the hut.

"Are you ready for this?" Justin jeers.

I am not smiling. *Ga-gung Ga-gung Ga-gung.* I legitimately feel like I am experiencing a heart attack. I lean on my trekking poles for support.

"Maybe I could just cross the river. It doesn't seem to be moving too quickly," I plead with a trace of hysteria.

"Oh, come on. You do know there are a million more of these on the South Island. You're going to have to get over it. Do you want me to take your poles? Your pack? That would help."

With my hands shaking, I turn over my poles. Justin makes the crossing first. He stops mid-river to give it a few bounces.

"See? It's really stable. It's really cool, actually." I swear I will punch him in the face if he so much as gives the bridge a wiggle when I step on it.

My turn comes. I clench both hands on the wispy wire sides and place one foot in front of the other on the aluminum plates. I push away visions of the scene in the movie *High Lane* when their swingbridge snaps.

"You got this babe!" Justin cheers. "Do you want me to come on the bridge and give it a bounce?"

I ignore Justin's mockery. My grip loosens and I gain trust in each forward step.

Like a shipwreck survivor reaching land, I almost cry when I step onto stationery ground. And, eleven hours after we started our day, we arrive at our sanctuary of man-made safety.

There are four Kiwis already settled in at Waite-waewae Hut, out for the weekend. They don't believe us when we tell them we came from Te Matawhai Hut today.

"That's bloody mad!" one of the guys remarks.

Justin pulls out our Sawyer water filter.

"You don't have to filter water; we're in a hut." I say.

Justin is paranoid about bacteria in water thanks to his Crohn's, and always insists on filtering. But our Sawyer pouch sprung a leak this week. We've duct taped it and have another one being sent to us, but the leak makes it a pain to use because we have to try not to squeeze too hard when pushing the water through.

"It's just too much of an effort tonight. I'm sure you're just as tired as I am and the last thing I want to do is wait ten minutes to filter one liter of water." It typically takes one minute, if that.

"Swingbridges make you nervous. Drinking unfiltered water makes me nervous," he looks at me sternly.

"I've read on the blogs that most hikers just drink unfiltered water from the huts and no one has had a problem," I assure him. "Just tonight, just until we replace our Sawyer pouch."

"Did you guys just drink the water from the tap?" Justin asks the Kiwis.

"Of course!" one exclaims. Justin acquiesces and goes outside to fill our water bottles.

He returns with only one filled.

"How do you explain this?" He shows me a small worm swimming in his water bottle. "Yeah, I'm going to take the extra time to filter our water."

After filtering, eating and cleaning up dinner, we both are ready to crash. I am curled deep in the folds of my down bag when I hear the Kiwis discussing what to do with their leftover dinner.

"Do you think I could offer to eat it?" I whisper to Justin.

"Are you still hungry?"

"Um yes. I just hiked for eleven hours," I slither out of my sleeping bag to make my *Oliver Twist* voice heard. "If you are planning to throw out your dinner leftovers, please don't. I will gladly eat them."

And in that instant, I serve the role of a human dustpan eating fresh broccoli, pasta and cheese from total strangers. This trail offers no shame.

After being coddled by the well-benched track through the Tarauas, the forest path leading to the suburbs of Wellington should be easy, but it is not. Our energy is low from our epic day before. We hike for three hours and cover three map miles. Finally, we see a sign that solves a mystery, revealing the trail miles are longer than the mapped miles.

A few hours later, we turn on our phone to see how much longer we have to go and realize we actually have cell service.

"Let's check our e-mail to see if we've heard from Leave No Trace." We hover around the small screen while the weak signal downloads all of our e-mails. Butterflies flutter in my stomach as I see a message from our Leave No Trace contact dated January 26, 2015.

"We received an extremely large pool of qualified applicants and, unfortunately, your team has not been selected to continue to the next round of the hiring process. You should know that you, unsurprisingly, made it to the top 25 teams in the application process out of over 125 applying teams."

Justin hugs me as I shed a few tears.

"We'll land on our feet," Justin squeezes my shoulders again. "We always do." He is right about that, and there's not much to say in this moment. We should know better about the futility of best-laid plans.

The biggest tradeoff to our "life less ordinary" is giving up a permanent address. There are a lot of in-between periods where we end up roaming while waiting for the next gig. We rented out our home and use it as a storage unit, but the key to making this life sustainable and giving us the financial freedom to be wanderers was paying off all debt and dwindling our bills to just health insurance and one cell phone. Work is necessary, but we get to choose specific jobs in the outdoor and hospitality industry all over the United States that gives us a little cash to get by, while more importantly broadening our horizons. People forget that often times, these oddball jobs come with housing, enabling us to keep our cost of living and overhead low. There is no way we could have taken six months off to hike if we hadn't budgeted or had a normal career or had children for that matter.

With Leave No Trace off the table and the rest of 2015 as a blank slate, we can start daydreaming about other possibilities. So many of our discoveries started with an open mind and the statement, "I don't know." The planner in me has definitely lost hours of sleep about where we'd live and work next, but Justin balances out my hysteria with his lofty dreams and fearlessness. And even though it is never a linear path, we always create our own happiness. Maybe we'll find a new location to be caretakers and/or managers. Maybe we'll live in a camper van and travel the country, picking up freelance writing to fill in the dry periods. If uncertainty is the first ingredient in adventure, then we have it in spades.

"Well, let's hike on," I finally say. "We'll apply for Leave No Trace again next year."

| 9 |

Windy Welly

Days 64-68: 57.8 miles

"Three, two, one!" shrieks a chubby Maori boy, about ten years of age.

In succession, twenty-two Maori boys jump from the State Highway One bridge twenty feet below into Pukerua Bay in Porirua.

Our Te Araroa tour through the suburbs of Wellington follows mostly paved roads, including more of State Highway One. In 2016, the Te Araroa Trust will have opened up a six-mile section replacing some of the highway walking around Wellington. Remembering that road walking is considerably less on the South Island, I enjoy our last bits of North Island culture.

Last night, on the edge of Porirua, we ate McDonalds for dinner and stumbled upon a wooded patch of land suitable for camping. The surrounding structures looked like relics of an old train station, but without the tracks.

We knocked on a few doors to no avail, deciding we wouldn't be intruding by sleeping on the edge of the large property overlooking the town below. From our hillside, we watched factory workers shut down for the evening and called it a night ourselves.

We were quickly reminded of our urban location when at 10 P.M., the factory's night shift came to life. I could still hear the beeping forklifts through my earplugs.

At the edge of the North Island, Wellington is the southernmost capital city in the world with the second most populous urban area in New Zealand behind Auckland. It horseshoes around the harbor with land and houses perched above on the abrupt hills, thanks to the city's position along an active geological fault. We pause to admire the vibrant succulent plants in the botanical gardens, stroll over train tracks and platforms, tiptoe through a cemetery and hug the tiny edge of the highway shoulders. Zigzagging the hilly city streets is dizzying and we often have to stop to consult our trail maps and notes. A few cars pull over to check on us.

"Are you on the Amazing Race?" one woman shouts out her car window.

Though it is only twenty-five miles, this last day of the North Island trek is long. Because of Wellington's location in the Roaring Forties (between the latitudes of forty and fifty degrees) and its exposure to the gusts blowing through the Cook Strait, it has the nickname "Windy Welly." We experience the first of this on Mount Kaukau overlooking the city with wind that could cut you in two.

As we take the last steps of our victory march, we climb through the coastal reserve and drop down into Shorland Park. Tasting the salty air again, I recall a quote from the philosopher Epictetus and it strikes me as the last sixty-five days of whipsaw emotions seep into my consciousness.

"Circumstances don't make the man; they reveal him to himself."

Any long-distance hike is going to teach you about yourself and your limits. This is why Justin and I are drawn to backpacking together. People don't realize the mental part of long-distance hikes is generally harder than the physical part.

Our abnormal life has zero boundaries—we work, eat, sleep and play together. For goodness sake, now we share a cell phone. It's a little hard to find oneself while being tethered to one another. Justin could tell me to relax all he wanted, but the unpredictability of this trail would accomplish the task on my terms. It would teach me how to roll with the punches at my own pace until it becomes a mindset that can be applied elsewhere. I needed to be assured that the twists and turns can transform into magical landings. I needed the reminder that the more we embark on the unknown, the braver we become to keep going on our life-less-ordinary journey. I needed to gain confidence in myself, not in the circumstance. I cannot control the circumstance, but can control my own confidence, and that's the most important thing going forward.

The rawness of the North Island's Te Araroa can only accentuate these results. Being only among hundreds who have walked the still-growing trail means we had to rely on one another like never before—making split-second, crucial decisions together and slamming up to the consequences of those choices without getting angry at each other. We are more at ease as partners and with the trail. Though there are times when I seriously questioned my sanity in choosing this adventure, I knew I was exactly where I should be.

There is a rock commemorating the end of the North Island section of Te Araroa. It so appropriately reads:

WALK THE PATH IN SAFETY, LOOK DEEPLY AND
LEARN FROM YOUR SURROUNDINGS

I drop my pack and collapse next to the sign. My eyes fall for a moment to my loose waistband, bare legs, hairy, dusted with dirt and speckled with a constellation of bruises and scratches. I wiggle my toes inside my boots, feeling the smattering of the remaining nail on my big toe. Tears threaten to stream down my face as I gaze north, the direction of a wild land that schooled, scorched and manipulated me. I turn slowly to the south and breathe in the beacon of accomplishment that awaits.

It is 6:30 P.M. on Friday, January 30, sixty-five days after we began at Cape Reinga at the top of the North Island. Our map tells us we have completed 1,047 miles, though we know we've walked more. The point is, finishing the North Island means we are more than halfway done with Te Araroa.

A family notices our paparazzi attempts to capture the moment at the sign.

"How ya goin?" the lady asks. "Whot's so special about this sign?"

We give them the brief version, as I am anxious to call Carole to come pick us up.

"Surry, did you say you wolked from the North Cape?" the man laughs. "That's a helluva grunt, ay? You must be gutted, ay?"

We launch into our wandering storyteller role and it's only moments before the couple offers us a place to stay tonight.

"That's awfully nice of you, but we actually made arrangements to stay with some folks we met in the bush while tramping who live here," I respond.

"Well where do they live? We can take you on over!"

"In the Karori neighborhood," I say, stealing a glance at Justin. With all the hospitality Carole and Tony are planning to provide, I am happy to ask one less thing of them.

I call Carole with news of getting a ride and she ends with, "I hope yar hungry and keen on eating; we have heaps of fush and chips waiting for you!"

The two days and three nights at Carole and Tony's house offer easy living. They allow us to come and go as we please and refuse to let us buy them a meal or pitch in with cooking. They turn over their basement to us and it provides all the luxuries of life at our disposal—bed, shower, Internet, and laundry (even a dryer). I feel so pampered and couldn't have asked for a better situation. Never wanting to put anyone out, I thank them every chance I can, but their Kiwi hospitality overshadows my internal dilemma.

Now that we know we don't have to be back in the states for the Leave No Trace job, we explore our options for booking our return flight. Our six-month visa was set to expire April 20, 2015. Justin started looking around for flights—wanting to find a deal, but also to see if we could visit another country on the way back, once again keeping the stoke alive. He found reasonable, one-way flights leaving New Zealand from Christchurch on April 20th that included a five-day stop in Sydney. To Australia we'd go!

"I know you have heaps of errands and catching up to do," Carole says, "but if you guys are interested, we'd love to take you snorkeling."

It does not take us long to say a resounding yes. When else would we have an opportunity to go snorkeling in New Zealand?

The four of us drive thirty minutes over to Makara Beach, a sparsely developed sea cove close to the shore of the Tasman Sea. Since there are only two wet suits and Tony is our expert diver, Carole, Justin and I alternate the other suit.

I dive into the crystal-clear water first, following Tony through the weaving seaweeds and tangled kelp thickets on the seabed. Hundreds of fish dart away from us as we swim through. The water is shallow, so I help myself along using the coral reef as a stabilizer.

Our goal is to collect paua for dinner. Paua is an edible snail mainly found in the seas around New Zealand. Tony uses his tools to pry the sea creatures, which are as large as his hand, from their hidden domains. He signals for me to try, but I am unsuccessful as its black, muscular foot remains stuck in place.

We resurface and Tony counts three paua shells in his bag. The shells mesmerize us with their striking blue, green and purple iridescence. I can see why people make jewelry and decorations out of the encasements.

I squeeze out of the wet suit to give Justin a turn.

"Is there anything in the water that can kill me?" he asks, alarmed.

"Well, just a bit of sting rays," Tony retorts. "Oh, and I guess sharks."

Justin grew up swimming in pools. I grew up swimming in lakes.

Tentatively, Justin follows Tony and they come back to the shore with three more paua. Tony and Carole go in once more. I rattle on about how awesome the experience is to Justin, while he admits he was just a little nervous swimming around the dark sea.

Back at Carole and Tony's house, we help with the shucking process to remove the foot from the shell, the same as you would for an oyster. Then, we dice the meat. I am surprised at how white the inside is compared to the black exterior. We leave the rest to Tony, who sautés the paua in butter and garlic until the white turns grey, and we go clean up for dinner.

There is a text from Marilyne checking in. She is now about five days behind us at the Makahika Outdoor Pursuits Centre with several other hikers, including Matteo, who just caught up to her. We give her beta about our experience in the Tarauas and wish her clear weather tidings. We are still hopeful we will reunite with them.

Justin asks me if I've seen some of the awards and medals on our hosts' shelves, as well as the pictures of Tony with different presidents. We know Tony's career was in the New Zealand Navy.

"I think he was something big in the Navy," Justin speculates. "I'll ask him over dinner."

Later in the evening, the four of us enjoy our Kiwi seafood delicacy served over toast as an appetizer, followed by lamb roast, kumara, green beans and corn. When Justin poses the question about Tony's career, Carole responds, "Go on Tony, don't be modest."

Turns out, Tony was the Chief of the Royal New

Zealand Navy until 2012. His rear admiral ranking is above a commodore and captain, equivalent to a major-general in the U.S. Army or Air Force. The man has his own Wikipedia page and we are staying under his roof.

Our last day in Wellington, we tour all six floors of Te Papa, New Zealand's free museum highlighting history, art and culture of the indigenous and non-indigenous people. The remains of the world's largest colossal squid, which was found in 2007 off the coast of Antarctica by a Kiwi fisherman, reside on permanent display at the museum.

On Monday, February 2, Carole drives us to the ferry terminal, where we board the Interislander freight at 8:30 A.M., which will take us from the North Island three hours across the Cook Strait to Picton, the entry to the South Island. The day we cross the Cook Strait is misty and cloudy, but not as tempestuous as it can be. We enjoy exploring the seven decks of the boat and watching the slideshow out the window as we thread through the picturesque Tory Channel and Queen Charlotte Sound.

Our noon arrival is timed perfectly with the kickoff of the SuperBowl XLIX in America. We secure bunks at a hostel and a seat at the bar to watch the New England Patriots win over the Seattle Seahawks in a close game.

| 10 |

The South Island Begins
Days 69-78: 165.6 miles

"To this cove Captain Cook made five visits while navigating the globe," I read the monument out loud to Justin. A second aquatic journey from Picton just dropped us at Ship Cove, where Captain James Cook first landed on January 15, 1770, to become the first European to step foot on New Zealand soil.

It is day sixty-nine and we are starting the South Island portion of the trek. Compared with the North Island, the South Island has far fewer people and more open spaces. We begin on the forty-mile Queen Charlotte Track down one of the arms of the Marlborough Sound from Ship Cove to Anakiwa. As soon as we set foot off the boat and onto the track, I realize we are in for a treat. The route is not one of New Zealand's Great Walks, but it is certainly heavily served and used. I am not tripping over any rocks or roots; the path is wide and thorn-free and the grades are gradual. Established campsites and lodges dot the route. There is a $12 per person fee to walk this section to help the private property owners maintain it, plus fees at the campgrounds, but frankly, if fees equal A+ track, I'd be willing to pay more of them.

The trail follows the curve of the inlets in the Marlborough Sounds, where the easiest—and sometimes only—access to the unspoiled coastline is often by boat. We enjoyed seaside scenery similar to this early in our trek up north in the Bay of Islands, but the constant route finding often obstructed the views.

For three days, we walk with ease and savor the aesthetic appeal of mountains and ocean. The bush-clad hills angle dramatically up and away from the aquamarine sea in the quiet nooks.

Soon enough, the deafening drum of the cicada calls and sultry, sticky heat makes us feel as if we are in the tropics and we dream of our next resupply stop in Havelock with its freezers and refrigerators.

"Has anyone told you about the weka?" an English chap buzzes at the established camp of Cowshed Bay, which looks more like a large gravel parking lot with covered picnic tables than a fee-based campground. There are eight people around the table; this feels crowded after having the entire North Island bush to ourselves. Hiking on the South Island is incredibly popular and tourists flock to the trails for day and weekend trips. In fact, many Te Araroa walkers opt only to do the South Island section.

"No," I reply, while pouring boiling water into our Italian Pasta with Beef dehydrated meal.

"Be careful. They are very cheeky birds, pilfering food straight from your hand. I put my granola bar down for one second, and it was gone in an instant!"

Easily mistaken for the kiwi birds, the weka are large, brown and flightless. Unlike the kiwi, though, the weka are out and about during the daylight and are attracted to human activity.

Suitably informed from that point on, we shoo their furiously running, little brown legs away anytime they get too close, trying our very best to Respect Wildlife, yet another Leave No Trace principle.

Visions of cold drinks pop into my head as we consider the mileage for the last day. It would be close to twenty-six miles to get us into Havelock. We decide to go for it and leave camp by 7:15 A.M.

By 6:30 P.M., we are sitting down at the Mussel Pot in Havelock, ordering the South Island's specialty of greenshell mussels. Endemic to New Zealand and one of the largest in the mussel family, the greenshell mussels are softer and milder in taste, without a briny or chewy texture. And, of course, we wash them down with cold beverages.

We opt to skip laundry given our time constraints, but wake early and allow ourselves a few hours in the morning to catch up on posting our blog and e-mails.

Included in town duties is a twenty-minute phone conversation I have to have with the Health Insurance Marketplace. They automatically renewed our 2015 health insurance plan unbeknownst to me, but the American-based plan has no use in New Zealand. I would rather save the monthly premium cost, and we'll enroll when we return to the United States. The phone call's reality check leaves me with a headache the size of an eighteen-wheeler truck switching gears every fifteen minutes, but it is another one of those life tasks that falls in my wheelhouse. Justin would have no idea how to approach this issue. Forever detail-oriented, I even put the wheels in motion to have our 2014 taxes filed while on the trail.

By 11 A.M., we are back on the trail with fully loaded backpacks, ready for the Richmond Range. The Queen Charlotte Track was merely a warm-up for the South Island and now we will confront the true nature of the trail again.

According to Te Araroa alumni, the Richmond Range is more intimidating than the Tarauas. Even though it is only a one hundred-mile section with a high point of 5,679 feet, it takes trampers an average of nine days to complete. The Richmond Range erupts up from the Earth like great monuments of rock, starting the backbone of the Southern Alps. The elevation changes are extreme and there is a good bit of above-treeline ridge walking. Weather can also be a nuisance, forcing backpackers to hunker down for days. Hikers one week in front of us encountered massive snow. Without any road access, it makes for a long stretch and full commitment.

Our trail notes are riddled with warnings like:
THE TRACK IS OFTEN INDISTINCT ON THE GROUND
Or, my personal favorite is this one:
THERE'S A RIVER CROSSING ON A ROCK CHUTE JUST ABOVE A FOUR-METER (TWELVE FOOT) WATER-FALL. THE WATER IS FLOWING FAST DOWN THE CHUTE AND IF YOU LOSE FOOTING, YOU GO OVER THE WATERFALL.

We carry ten days' worth of food and pack an extra punch of courage to play it safe.

On the road walk into the Richmond Range, a Kiwi

couple in a campervan pulls over to see if we want a ride to the trailhead. We decline, but spend a few minutes chatting. Max and Lyn are from Christchurch and are still tramping in their seventies. In fact, Max has completed the whole Te Araroa in sections. If Justin and I live that long, it is the active life we covet. We exchange information, as they tell us if we come through Christchurch, they would be happy to host us.

Initially, we walk through the rimu and beech forest lined by the Pelorus River, famous because of its cameo in the *The Lord of the Rings* and *The Hobbit* movies and as clear to the bottom as teal-tinted saran wrap.

Aside from abundant bellbirds and tomtits, the birds ubiquitous to the North Island forests seem nonexistent in their counterparts of the South Island. Instead, an orchestra of buzzing wasps replaces birdsong.

We notice the trees have a furry look to their bark, until we realize the fur is buzzing. 2015 is a mast year, meaning there are high levels of seed production by the beech trees, not only contributing to an exploding population of wasps, but also of mice and rats too. The wasp and rodent reputations precede themselves. I heard records of twenty-one wasp stings for one person and huts overrun by pesky four-legged critters.

The game-changer for this section—and pretty much the whole South Island going forward—are the huts, which are purposely placed every four hours or so. Our first sleepover is in Rocks Hut. We both collapse in a sweaty, red-faced heap under our heavy backpack loads. Just as we had suspected, we will no longer be alone on the South Island. We share the hut with four other people, all out for an overnight hike.

My favorite thing about the huts is not the fact they provide refuge from inclement weather. It is the visitor book. The Department of Conservation uses the Intentions Books to keep track of backpackers for safety purposes and to record usage. Huts are free for day use, but overnight stays often cost. They use a ticket and a pass system. Justin and I purchased a six-month backcountry hut pass for our trek.

Across two pages in the books, there is a line for gathering information from each party. The columns collect the date, number of nights in the hut, backcountry hut pass number, hometown/country, trip intentions, weather conditions and comments/observations.

On the Appalachian Trail, there were shelter logs. Forest officials similarly use the books for the partial registry purpose of lost or missing hikers, but the Appalachian Trail notebooks with blank pages leave a lot of room for hikers to fill with creativity. The shelter logs act as a living history of thru hiker culture and could keep us entertained for hours each evening.

In New Zealand's hut books, there is not as much prose or artwork, but it is still a treasure trove of tidbits from all the Te Araroa hikers in front of us. I peruse the trip intentions column, which highlights all the "TA" walkers. I immediately search for our friends, Clara and BJ, who hiked the trail in 2013, as well as our friends, Erin and Paul, who just finished hiking the South Island this month. Clara, BJ, Erin and Paul sign the registers with their American trail names—Country Mouse, Shadow, Fern Toe and Thor. We actually know them better by their trail names.

We met Erin, or "Fern Toe," and Paul, or "Thor," on the

Appalachian Trail. Fern Toe had been a southbounder like us who we were stalking via the shelter books. We finally met her in Virginia and ended up completing the trail on the same day. She met Thor, a ridge runner, on the Appalachian Trail, and now they are happily married.

As for Clara, or "Country Mouse," and BJ, or "Shadow," they were northbounders on the Appalachian Trail. We exchanged pleasantries in passing on the trail in Massachusetts. Clara kept a blog that I periodically checked, and it quickly became my favorite when I realized they were hiking Te Araroa in 2013. They are like-minded nomads and adventurers, so our friendship blossomed as we continue to meet up in the most random places.

Your trail name is the pseudonym that others know you by. It is your story—your identity.

On the Appalachian Trail, Justin earned the name "Deal" because he loves scoring bargains—especially on outdoor gear—and telling people about the discounts. In 2003, Justin purchased a pair of Mountain Hardwear zip-off hiking pants on a pro-deal while working as a guide in Denali National Park. These pants had nearly four thousand miles on them from the Appalachian Trail, this hike and others, but the first thing he needs to share with others is the discounted cost.

My trail name is "Steadee" because I lead Justin in a slow and steady pace. Justin is a much faster hiker than I am, but if he were leading, we wouldn't be hiking together. On our thru hike of the Appalachian Trail, I was almost always in front. It made me uncomfortable at first, to always have him clipping at my heels. But my pacing kept us more in sync.

I wonder if trail names will ever catch on here in New

Zealand.

I continue to scroll through the more recent hut book entries and look for Ole, Nadav and Goni, whom we had met on the North Island and who were several days in front of us. Just a few days ahead are a bunch of hikers we have yet to meet: Apple Pie, Greenleaf and Burrito, a trio from the states, Serina from Canada, Nicolas from France, Patrick from the United States, Eef from Belguim, PJ from Norway, Andrew from Canada and David from the United States. I wonder if we will ever catch up to them. I am also drawn to names from the blogs I am following, particularly the extremely informative and detailed "Restless Kiwi," Kirstine, and the American power couple, Kenzie and Cam. There is also an entry from an Irish couple, Alan and Lauren, alerting people about a "Hiker Trash St. Patrick's Day Party" in Queenstown on March 17. I make a mental note, but that also feels far away, as it is only February 7.

I sign us into the visitor book for Rocks Hut. The date is February 7, 2015. I scribble our hut pass number and that we are from Colorado, USA. I record perfect weather conditions and for comments and observations, I write "beautiful trail today, but swingbridges will be the death of me." We crossed five swingbridges today.

Green and yellow Department of Conservation signs naming the hut and mileage make an appearance at every shelter junction. It is almost alarming to have so much signage and established track to follow. However, the mileage on the signs never match the mileage clocked by our GPS, nor the mileage listed on our maps and trail notes. Our GPS never fails to record more distance. It dumbfounds us how a government agency and trail organization could be wrong about the mileage, but I have faith that my satellite-enabled tracker is telling the truth.

On our fourth day in the Richmond Range at Starveall Hut, we wake above the clouds. The Maori name for New Zealand is Aoetaroa, which translates to "land of the long white cloud," and it seems so appropriate from our viewpoint. With a plan to make it the twelve miles up and over the challenging terrain of Mount Rintoul, we start hiking by 7:15 A.M.

Among the alpine vegetation include little mounds of succulents and vegetable sheep, which amazingly only grows one cell per year. We leapfrog a young and loud group of five German hikers. A father and son within the group are southbound on Te Araroa, while the rest are just out for a few days.

Under sinister skies, we reach our first scree climb over Little Rintoul. My anxiety goes from subdued to worried to completely panic-striken in the matter of a minute. The five swingbridges we crossed yesterday are child's play compared with scree.

Scree is a mass of broken and loose rock fragments resulting from landslides that bury entire mountain slopes. The granulation and type of rock—stones, talus, slate, shale, clay, tuff, basalt, granite—determine how much the surface dislodges under your feet. On the grueling uphill battle, you take one step forward, four steps back. The downhills became ski runs. Without any trees, there is nothing to grasp onto. And with only orange poles dispersed about the hill, the path is up to you.

The talus cracks under my feet like broken glass. I stab my trekking poles into the ground for futile stability. I am thankful for the new boots we just received in the mail in

Wellington, giving me a little traction.

We reach the summit of Little Rintoul at 5,390 feet. I am relieved, but it is temporary. Through the thick cloak, I can hardly make out our dodgy, one-mile ridgeline path that will drop down a bit, then rise back up to the summit of Mount Rintoul at 5,679 feet. Even from far away, I can tell that the width of the path is shatteringly close to either edge.

My heart takes a swan dive out of my chest and plummets downhill with the loose rocks. I whirl around to Justin, "I need to stop for a break."

"Take some deep breaths," Justin lays his hand on my shoulder. "Do you want some gummy worms? I opened them yesterday."

I sit down on a rock and chew on one, hoping the sugar may settle my nervous stomach. I never used to be afraid of heights. In my twenties, I went skydiving twice and jumped off a seventy-foot cliff three times. But, the combination of knife edges and unsteady surfaces puts me in a full-on hysteria.

I look ahead. Like a photo slideshow, the fog has shrouded in the mountains again. I stand up slowly. The timing is now. Walking through the clouds will prohibit me from pondering my fall off the thousand-foot drop on either side. Instead, I can concentrate on putting one foot in front of the other on my six-inch-wide walkway.

"We'll just take it really slow," Justin reassures. "Do you want me to go first?"

I avoid speaking—thinking tears may burst out—and just nod my head yes.

I travel like a limp locomotive behind Justin. He stops often, looking behind and putting out his arm for assistance when we have to balance on our toes around a huge boulder blocking the already narrow path.

We take another break at Mount Rintoul. With one gauntlet over, I turn my eyes to the second ordeal—a thousand-foot steep and trackless descent over loose rubble back into the woods. I instruct Justin to go at his own pace, knowing my turtle progress will only prompt him to egg me on. I blink and Justin is a football field ahead of me.

Using my best mountain goat skills, I plod down the slope, gripping my poles tightly to steady my clumsy footing. I try valiantly to stay vertical, my eyes wedged open assessing the footholds and my knees wobbling like Elvis. Squashing the part of my brain that is screaming, "you're going to slide down this mountain to your death," I decide the best method is to instead travel down on my butt, clinging on the unsteady rocks.

The sound of rockfall behind me cues me to brace for an avalanche.

"Thees iz fun!" one of the German guys from earlier sneers as he bounds past me. There isn't enough calmness in my face to muster a smile, so I just scowl. Two more of the Germans rockslide past me in the same manner a few minutes later.

Justin is waiting for me at the treeline.

"I don't think it is much farther to the hut," he acknowledges. "We should probably just sleep in the tent tonight since the hut only sleeps six and there are at least five that we know of."

"That's fine by me."

"Plus," Justin adds as we walk through the beech trees, "I'm sure there will be some snorers in this group."

Snorers in huts are distracting, like cooing babies in a church. Earplugs are a necessity.

Sure enough, at the six-man Rintoul Hut, there are a total of ten people for the night. It all works out when four of us camp outside. Justin and I eat our Persian Chicken Stew dehydrated meal cramped in the hut with the others to be social—and because it is raining out—then retire to our snore-free tent.

My watch reads thirty-seven degrees in the tent at 7:15 A.M. Justin snuggles tighter in his forty-degree blanket and murmurs, "Five more minutes." After such warm temperatures on the North Island, we realize that the huts may have an added benefit of warmth at these higher elevations.

An early morning climb out of the morning wreath of fog brings us to more ridge walking—much less daunting than yesterday's above-treeline walk. All day, we crisscross paths with the hut dwellers. Their plan is to stay in Mid Wairoa Hut. Not wanting to battle the crowds, we privately decide we should push for Top Wairoa Hut, just five miles further.

The day goes smoothly and we smash the miles, passing through the fairytale forests with cartoon-like orange and purple toadstools around every corner. I half expect a pint-sized gnome to pop out and wish us well.

It is those last five miles to Top Wairoa Hut that turn schizophrenic. "Sidling" is a common Kiwi tramping term that means "to negotiate a steep slope by moving transversely." I had seen it throughout our trail notes, but to sidle never seemed too problematic. So, when this last bit reads that it follows the river and "involves a lot of sidling, at times on steep terrain and numerous river crossings," I think nothing of it.

This chunk of sidling offers a whole new flavor. It literally means shimmying along a crumbling precipice with your stomach to the wall because the path is not wide enough for your boot, just your tiptoe. I tread lightly, as my eroding margin for error could be my last step.

In between the sidling—or suicidling—we drop from the outcrops into the gorge where the faint path darts from one side of the river to the other. With the low water level, we are able rock hop all of the crossings. Even the crossing above the twelve-foot waterfall is benign.

We desperately try to find a camp spot, forgoing our hut plans. The rocky landscape is uninviting, so we keep trudging along. After about three hours from the last hut—when we surely think we should be at Top Wairoa Hut—a cliff halts our forward progress. Across the stream to our left, we see another cliff. There doesn't appear to be a likeness of a trail on that side, so we crank our heads toward the crag and notice an orange pole five hundred feet above us.

"It looks impossible, but I think the trail is up there," Justin shakes his head. "Let me go up a little and see what I see."

I let him scramble as I continue to scrutinize the rocky landscape across the stream.

"Yep," he bellows down to me fifteen minutes later, "the hut is up here."

At five foot, five inches, I am not tall enough for Te Araroa. Hand over foot, I struggle up the perilous rocky wall. Contact with the ground remains tenuous for the entire fifteen minutes it takes me to reach the top.

Painted bright orange, Top Wairoa Hut gleams on top

of the embankment. There is already one British woman, Caroline, inside, who is doing a section hike and came from the last hut today. I convince Justin we should stay inside the hut today. Though it only takes us less than five minutes to erect our tent, I lack the energy for the task. Plus, Caroline surely doesn't snore.

"Tonight is a two-dinner night," I declare to Justin. With five days of food left in our provisions and less than three days to town, we need not worry about running out. We never eat enough to support the near-five-thousand calories we are expending daily, especially Justin, who has more muscle mass and a metabolism that burns calories just looking at food.

One of the Beef Stroganoff dehydrated meal packages I am cooking is missing the oxygen absorber packet, but I still prepare it.

"This doesn't look normal, babe," Justin complains about the Beef Stroganoff. "And it tastes kind of weird," he adds while smacking his lips. Normally creamy white in color, the contents are distinctly darker than the other pouch.

"Um, yeah, it was missing the oxygen absorber," I reveal.

"Oh God, I can't eat this," he pushes it aside.

"Here, have mine," I hand over my pouch. "I'll eat it. I don't want to carry it out and my stomach is less sensitive than yours."

"Really? We can just pack it out and share this one," he offers while I take a bite and grimace.

"I'll just eat what I can." Despite my extreme hunger, every bite tastes chalkier and chalkier.

While choking down a good majority of Beef

Stroganoff, we commiserate about the trail conditions with Caroline, who is new to backpacking. In the hut book, one entry says, "I came here to walk, not die." We concur.

An hour later, a man with wild hair, wearing shorts and a tank top reminiscent of the 1980s, strides through the door. Hannes, from Germany, is northbound on Te Araroa. His energy bounces off the tin walls like a tennis ball. He speaks like boiling water, his words spilling over each other about the upcoming terrain. I am disturbed hearing the terms "knife edges," "scree," and "sidling," multiple times.

Rod, one of the non-German Rintoul Hut dwellers from yesterday, lunges through the door at dusk. At seventy years old and hair as white as the alpine flowers, we are shocked he made it the fifteen miles. But he is a Kiwi, and Kiwis are known for being hardcore in their tramping skills.

"I wonted to get ahead of the bubble," he remarks. Rod tells us that there is a bubble of hikers in front of us and the bubble we met behind us, so he really wanted to get to the small village of Saint Arnaud before the weekend mobs. Overall, the South Island is notably more congested than the North Island, so we started to get in the habit of calling ahead to hostels when possible, although planning and trail walking do not exactly go hand in hand. Before entering the Richmond Range, we sent an e-mail to one of the lodges in Saint Arnaud asking about availability on Thursday, Friday or Saturday in their bunk room for backpackers. Our estimates suggest we will arrive Friday, so next time we have a signal, we plan to check on their reply.

With five people in the six-person hut, this feels a little

too cramped, but I am adamant about not having to set up our tent. Justin presses the idea, but eventually unenthusiastically complies with my demands. He climbs on his upper bunk, as his theory is that the mice won't bother him up there.

Turns out, Top Wairoa Hut has enough mice to feed a full-capacity shelter if hikers get stranded for days.

I wake to rustling and pattering feet first. Ears perked and eyes wide open, my forehead is tickled by something furry running across. Thwarting my impulse to scream, I sit up and turn on my headlight. Dark beady eyes at the end of my sleeping bag stare back, then scamper off.

"I've been listening to them for hours," Justin whispers from up above in an I-told-you-so tone, hearing my commotion.

"Are they getting into our packs or food bags?" I worry.

"I haven't gotten up to check," Justin speaks softly.

I go and shake our bags, which are hanging from the rafters, but nothing seems to be in or on them.

Caroline turns on her headlight from another bunk.

"They have been zipping around me all night. I haven't slept at all," she complains.

The three of us spend a few minutes on high alert, darting our headlight beams in the direction of any crinkling or scurrying we hear. Both Hannes and Rod continue to snore with vigor.

"Should we go set up our tent outside?" I ask Justin.

"I don't know," he signs. "I'm going to just put in my earplugs and hope to catch some sleep."

After another crimping noise near Caroline's bag, she gets up to rummage through her things.

Justin jumps a little as one crawls over his sleeping bag.

"Whot in bloody hell is all the noise?" Rod blurts out.

"There are mice all over the place," Caroline explains. Hannes continues to rip up the sound waves with his heavy breathing.

"Well some of us are trying to bloody sleep," he groans and lets his sleeping bag swallow his head.

As soon as the sun rises, we gather our things to start hiking, cranky from sleep deprivation. Caroline confirms that a mouse chewed through her water bottle. Our belongings remain unscathed.

Top Wairoa Hut becomes an orange dot in the distance as we climb up to another ridgeline.

Seeing we have a cell signal, we check our messages. The lodge e-mailed to say they only have one of their more expensive motel rooms available for Thursday, but nothing at all for Friday, Saturday or Sunday.

It is Wednesday. We still have thirty miles to get to the village.

"I think we can do it," Justin rallies. "We'll tent camp tonight somewhere between huts."

I start to question our decision when we encounter a monster scree slope. However, this time we are to walk across it, not up or down. I combat my nerves and negotiate the terribly eroded footpath, watching as our silhouettes stretch long below us in the sunlight.

The body of land gradually transforms under our feet, demonstrating New Zealand's sharp, stunning contrasts. In the Red Hills, we are wandering through ophiolites, rock rich with iron and magnesium that has been lifted up by the tectonic plates and fault lines. The mix of crystals, rocks and minerals sends cinnamon spires vaulting skyward. It is like walking on sandpaper, and while the stable footing is a nice change, catching my bare skin on it makes me less appreciative.

The day feels long in the sizzling heat of the ozone-free, scorching sun. I already feel the sleep deprivation from the preceding night taking a toll. We lounge for an extended lunch break at Hunters Hut, which was rebuilt in memory of two Department of Conservation workers who died in the nearby Bush Edge Hut when a flash flood wiped them out in 1995. We take another break at Porters Hut. I read again in the Department of Conservation Intentions Book about this hiker trash party on Saint Patrick's Day in Queenstown and wonder again about our timing. We push ourselves to go extra miles, putting us closer to St. Arnaud.

We scramble in and out of small stream beds. Given the fate of the Department of Conservation workers, Justin searches for a higher camp spot, but they are slim pickings. He finds one clearing off the trail that is barely enough room for the tent body, let alone the rainfly. In our tent, on a mattress of loose rocks and dirt, we keep our fingers crossed for no rain.

With the moon just an eyelash, we enjoy a dome of stars and constellations not seen in the Northern Hemisphere, including our first clear identification of the Southern Cross, finally, on day seventy-seven.

We wake up wet from dew the next morning and uncomfortable from a night spent rolling into each on the ever-so-slight hill we didn't notice when setting up.

When our lethargic legs finally reach the village of St. Arnaud at 2 P.M., the heat and malnutrition of our seven-day tramp through the Richmond Range takes its toll and the higher-priced motel room option seems worth every penny.

| 11 |

Glacier-Fed Lakes and
Snow-Capped Mountains
Days 79-88: 159.5 miles

"Happy Hallmark holiday," Justin jokes, handing me a package of powdered donuts for breakfast. He pulls out a honey bun from our food bag for himself.

These special treats came in a care package sent by my mom to St. Arnaud. Though the village is right on Te Araroa, there is only a tiny country store with overpriced cheese and muesli, so I am grateful we sent a pre-arranged package of provisions to ourselves.

As for my mom's parcel, I had given her a few suggestions of what to include. Flavored oatmeals, honey buns and powdered donuts are trail breakfast favorites for us. However, Kiwi brands of oatmeal have been less appealing and individually packaged pastries are nonexistent here in New Zealand—at least in the fifteen grocery stores we've shopped—so breakfast has come up short for us.

I also put on my mom's list "pretzel M&Ms." She sent a package of plain M&Ms and a bag of Utz pretzels. I give her an "A" for effort.

Yesterday, we left St. Arnaud with packs bursting at the seams from our extra treats and seven days' worth of supplies in case the weather turns sour for our next section.

After semi-circling Lake Rotoiti to enter Nelson Lakes National Park, we wake up on Valentine's Day in the John Tait Hut with six other individuals. Compared with the cozy eight-person huts in the Richmond Range, this thirty-person hut likens to a boutique hotel.

The sign outside the hut is foreboding.

ARE YOU PREPARED FOR TRAVERS SADDLE?

Travers Saddle sits at approximately 5,900 feet, but the roughly two-thousand-foot climb would be spread over five miles. I'm thinking the sign is more hyperbolic than anything.

In any case, if Valentine's Day is for sentiments then it is only fitting that we declare our true love for Nelson Lakes National Park all day long. The spacious huts and fantastic mountain views under clear skies lure us to take extended snack and lunch breaks. Unambiguous trails liberate us to soak in everything, particularly the waterfalls thundering down like gigantic spouts into blissful pools surrounded by mossy rocks. The bewitching combination of beech tree forests and meadows peppered by subalpine flowers once again mimic a fairytale. We cannot stop saying "wow." Justin is not even fazed when a dreaded wasp stings him on his chest.

At Blue Lake Hut, we are joined by several weekenders—not surprisingly—couples, probably due to the Valentine's Day holiday. We cook up a new Backpackers Pantry meal from our food box we mailed ourselves to St. Arnaud; Fettuccine Alfredo could possibly be a new favorite to put in the books and replace our old favorite, Beef Stroganoff, ruined by the missing oxygen packet.

I flip through the hut book to see people writing about contaminated water at Blue Lake Hut.

"I fished a dead rat out of the water tank," someone writes.

I decide not to tell Justin this tidbit, but am happy we replaced our Sawyer Water Filter pouch and can continue our habit of always filtering water.

Three guests roll in right at dark. It turns out they are Apple Pie, Greenleaf and Burrito. I have been following this American trio in the Intentions Books since the Richmond Range and my suspicions about their trail names and strongly written opinions about Te Araroa are confirmed: these three have quite a few trails under their hip belts.

Turns out Apple Pie and Greenleaf are both Triple Crowners, having hiked the three big trails in the United States—Appalachian, Pacific Crest and Continental Divide Trails—as well as many others. Justin and I also hope to someday become Triple Crowners. We spend time with the three chatting about the differences between Te Araroa and trails in the United States, one being that no one uses trail names in New Zealand.

Given that it is thirty-eight degrees in the hut when we wake at 6:45 A.M., I heat up our granola, something we rarely do out of pure laziness, even with oatmeal. We sport our poof jackets for the morning walk past Blue Lake.

Blue Lake has the clearest water in the world, but this morning it resembles a sheet of blue velour in the shadows of the mountains.

It is here that the great history of the area reveals itself. New Zealand's most vigorous sculptor has been glaciers of past ice ages, scouring out deep valleys, leaving remnant podocarp forest and carving blocks of rock into jagged peaks that make up the ecological puzzle of the Southern Alps. It will become the norm during the subsequent weeks that we climb in and out of valleys full of glacier-fed, tranquil mountain lakes surrounded by eternally snow-capped summits. Pure bliss, I call it.

We climb our first natural moraine that dams the flashy and Caribbean-colored Lake Constance, sparkling from the rising sun. At the bottom, the impressive cirque of Waiau Pass at 6,200 feet overshadows Lake Constance. To reach Waiau Pass, we travel a poled-avalanche chute. The orange metal stakes are zigzagged—for what reason I don't know, other than providing a slalom course. Thankfully, we boss through the vertigo-inducing slope and enjoy a snack break among the leftover patches of ice wedged in between the rocks. A worrying number of trampers have disappeared from Waiau Pass, but clear weather and visibility make us feel safe and sound.

We follow the avalanche gully south using hand-over-hand descent—not enough that you need technical skills, just enough to imitate monkeys climbing over lumpy boulders. The rock debris bulldozed by age-old glaciers and tetonic turmoil create frantic-looking landforms. You can tell this side sees the violent weather and instability, as the orange poles are twisted like they had been wilted by the sun, but in fact it is because of winter avalanches.

We catch up to Apple Pie and Greenleaf, who are taking a break on a rocky terrace. Together, we descend the last bluffs to the Waiau River. The trio had been flip-flopping their Te Araroa route, so they have already done much of the South Island and are in the homestretch of completing it. We perk up our ears for solid advice from the seasoned pros.

"The worst part going south is the tussock," Greenleaf warns. This is not the first time I've heard hoopla about tussock, but from the patches we encountered up north, our initial impression leaves us thinking it is beautiful and harmless.

"Tussock is the ubiquitous desert grass that makes you want to burn every clump you see," Greenleaf explains. "Tussock makes walking tiring, difficult and painful." I still couldn't quite visualize why everyone thought it was so evil and wonder how tussock could be worse than the mud we endured on the North Island.

Apple Pie and Greenleaf jump ahead to catch Burrito at our last river crossing of the day. Justin and I had been taking our boots off and going barefoot because there were only a few, even though the frigid glacial water leaves us shivering.

We continue to follow the river in a valley route historically used by Southern Maori tribes to transport West Coast jade to Northern Maori tribes for trading. Though the Caroline Bivvy two-bunk shelter is unoccupied by people when we stroll up, we decide the resident rats would overrun the cramped tin shack and old canvas bunks, oozing with charm and terror in equal measures.

Tent camping on the grassy flats down river is a more desirable sleeping arrangement. By 2017, a new ten-person hut will replace this little hovel and meet more of the needs of the popular route, thanks to an anonymous donation to Te Araroa Trust.

A few miles later, we find a nice spot to set up our rat-free shelter. However, a dark cloud of other intruders appearing from nowhere joins us. Within seconds, the sandflies kamikaze the smallest bits of exposed skin. Setting up camp in record time, we throw everything inside the tent for protection, including ourselves. Instead of risking going anemic from the sandflies—who are now engulfing the tent walls—we risk burning down our house by cooking inside. Once the sandflies have gone to sleep, I step outside to use the bathroom and find a platinum crescent moon forming a half of a parenthesis cradled in the branches of the surrounding beech trees.

Another thirty-seven-degree morning keeps us from emerging until 8:45 A.M. Overnight frost painted the long grass as silver as an old man's hair. We appreciate the mellow ramble across the plains, but are drenched and chilled from the rime on the high grass. Eventually, the sun dries everything out and a lack of shade in the glaciated landscape breaks us into a sweat. Deep valleys funnel off from our straight track, but we continue ahead. We write "2000K" in the dirt and take a picture, marking a milestone of two-thirds of the trail completed.

After seventeen miles of grassy flats enclosed by native beech forest crawling up the high ranges, we reach Anne River Hut in the afternoon and call it a day. Anne River Hut has more windows than walls, three separate rooms and is bounded on all sides by views of thrusting spires of naked rock. This very exposed hut could be sweltering on the hottest of days, but today, it is my paradise. I spend much of the afternoon stalking other Te Araroa hikers via the Intentions Book, mentally ticking off my list. All alive. All accounted for. The Irish couple leaves another reminder about the Saint Patrick's Day party in Queenstown. I start to do the math and realize we could actually make it there—or at least close—in time.

We hear another hiker roll in late, after we are already tucked into one of the rooms, almost asleep. In the morning, we learn that it is Kevin from California. We met Kevin briefly in the village of St. Arnaud a few days ago and knew he was southbound on Te Araroa.

We leave by 8 A.M. and Kevin catches us at Boyle Flat Hut, where we are eating lunch. In his late thirties like us, Kevin is full of adventure and introspection; his ebullience is contagious. He is halfway through his goal to hike one hundred miles on all seven continents. One hundred miles was just not enough for New Zealand, which is why he is planning to do the approximately eight hundred miles of the South Island portion of Te Araroa. We decide to hike the remaining nine miles to Boyle Outdoor Center together.

"Hey," Kevin starts. "What did you mean, Patrice, when you wrote 'excited about Boyle Village' in the hut book and put village in quotes?"

"Our friends who just finished the South Island warned us to lower our expectations for any services," I explain sympathetically.

"Well, I know these towns have been small, but I'm hoping for at least a burger!"

"Hate to be the bearer of bad news, but Boyle Village

is nothing. I don't know why they call it a village in the trail notes. Boyle Outdoor Center, where we all sent our mail drops, is the only establishment there. It is a kids' camp, of sorts, although I heard they sometimes let you shower and sleep there. I think it just depends if they have programs going on. We plan to retrieve our package and move on."

"So, no burger?" Kevin pleads.

"No burger."

We arrive around 4 P.M. to Boyle Village, or rather, a cluster of camp buildings part of Boyle Outdoor Center. There is a flurry of activity, kids running around. The employees appear weary of hikers, so we tread lightly.

We leave our iPhones to charge for at least a few minutes while we disappear among the backs of the buildings to sort through our packages.

Clearly Justin and I thought Boyle Village was actually a town with a store when we packed our box back in Auckland before starting the trail. The contents include four oatmeals, three tunas, one package of beef jerky, one cup of soup, one package of dried apricots, one package of honey roasted peanuts, four granola bars, four packages of Honey Stinger organic chews, one package of Sour Patch Kids, four drink mixes and one bar of chocolate. This is meant to feed two extremely hungry hikers for five days. For some reason, we packed nine dehydrated dinners in this parcel, which adds to the three we have left over from the last section. Dinner for breakfast? And lunch? And dinner?

"Um, we're going to die of starvation," Justin panics.

"I heard this place has a little store sometimes stocked for hikers. Let's go ask and see what we can buy," I reassure him.

The store is a closet. It seems to carry a lot of leftover hiker box supplies, including an abundance of dried peas, and canned goods from the outdoor program, most of which are expired. We purchase $10 worth of food—crackers, chips and two cokes. We could hitch to nearby Hamner Springs—which a lot of hikers do—but we agree we will survive.

Justin spots a small cake and asks, "How much is that?"

The woman pulls it out, only to find that it is expired and a mouse has chewed on the packaging a little bit. The cake, though, is intact and has no mold, yet.

"I can't sell you this," the woman abhors.

"But are you going to throw it out?" Justin asks.

"Of course!" she protests.

"Please don't. I want it and I am starving," Justin begs. "You don't understand."

Still leery, she hands over the package.

At the carpark across the street, we devour one meal each, as well as the entire cake and set up camp for the night. The temperatures down in this valley are a little warmer than they have been, so we opt to leave our tent doors open, a decision that leaves our bags soaked from the overnight dew.

Kevin sticks with us as we continue to trek through expansive basins scooped out by glaciers and hugged by ominous peaks. We pass Lake Sumner, the largest lake on the South Island. With barely a breath of wind, our days on this mostly flat and fast section expose us to the sweltering sun.

The three of us stop at an unnamed hot springs highlighted in our trail notes. A Department of

Conservation sign reads:

HEALTH WARNING

AMOEBIC MENINGITIS IS FATAL AND CAUSED BY
WATER ENTERING NASAL PASSAGES.

DO NOT IMMERSE HEAD.

"Who would go under?" Justin shakes his head.

While stripping down to our undies, the sandflies gnaw at us—especially Kevin for some reason—like we are in a torture chamber. Sweet relief comes when we dip in, but the water is so hot, we only sink up to our waists.

After a short-lived soak thanks to the armada of sandflies and unbearable water temperature, we head to Hurunui No. 3 Hut for the night. We had seen helicopters flying over in the hut's direction. We thought it could be a hunting party or a Department of Conservation work crew. Either way, we hoped they had extra food.

It is the latter and thankfully, there is ample room for us in the sixteen-person hut. Three Te Araroa hikers I've been stalking in the books are also at the rustic hut—Patrick from the United States, Eef from Sweden and PJ from Norway. Eef and PJ met while working as guides in Sweden, then met Patrick on the trail way up north.

All three are in their twenties, contributing to a common trend in thru hiking. While age is about as relevant as the color of your socks, a typical thru hiker is either in their twenties, fresh out of school, or nearing retirement age, both of which have more time available for a thru hike. Of the eighteen Te Araroa thru hikers we've met so far—like Matteo and Ole—most have been under thirty. Being in our late thirties, Kevin, Justin and I are a rarity, having abandoned our careers for extended time off. Even so, nothing equalizes people better than stripping away all the comforts and being thrown into unfamiliar territory.

True to our hope, the Department of Conservation workers put down a plate of nachos in front of the six of us, only to watch it disappear five seconds later.

Patrick comments on Justin's updated Gregory Baltoro backpack. He has an older version, and the plastic mounting bracket in the shoulder strap had snapped.

"Can I play around with it?" Justin asks. Patrick happily passes it over as Justin pulls out paracord from our first aid kit.

"They fixed the Hubble Space Telescope with paracord," Justin brags. "So, if it can fix that, it can certainly fix a backpack."

Eef, PJ and I dodge the MacGyver gear clinic and sit on the bunks to chat. I find Eef to be a breath of fresh air. Not only is she another female, but she boasts of love for the trail. As a first-time thru hiker, she thinks Te Araroa is the bee's knees. She does not want the trail to end. I am the first to admit I am sometimes a Negative Nelly about the trail, so I soak up her blinding optimism as much as I can.

Then, she offers me some of her chocolate.

"Really?" I could never share my chocolate with anyone, not even my husband.

"Eat more, carry less!" she insists and hands me a package of Whittaker's to pick from.

I take Justin's advice and opt for a middle bed among the triple-stacked bunks, given the rumors about mice. This is a controlled area where the Department of Conservation does not try to poison the rodents and rather studies their impact.

As if the Department of Conservation workers were

trying to test the mice, they left food scraps and dirty dishes strewn about the hut, all while they tent camped outside. We had politely asked them to clean up before retiring to our bunks, but they seemed only to move around dishes. Since there was no opportunity for a conversation, Leave No Trace's authority of the resource guidelines, which focuses on polite education that explains the why instead of using enforcement power, told us to just leave it be.

I lay as still as a soldier with my back flat on the rubber mattress, my eyes focused on the bunk above me. Meanwhile, I hear mice doing somersaults from the roof to the bunks creeping closer and closer.

"Do you hear them?" Justin whispers.

"Yep," I reply smugly.

Not wanting to repeat a Top Wairoa Hut experience, I shove my earplugs in. Soon, my careful study of the ceiling succumbs to the backs of my eyelids.

The next afternoon, we part ways with Eef, PJ and Patrick, who are planning a shorter day than we are. Justin, Kevin and I rise from the valley over a three-thousand-foot pass in a nice change of pace, but then travel back down and follow the river, crossing it several times via foot and bridge. My fear of swingbridges—now that we've crossed more than twenty of them—has a different quality now. It does not incapacitate me or interfere with my competence. It becomes the natural, healthy fear one needs for survival.

I revert a little bit when I encounter our next crossing. It is a three-wire swing bridge. There is no netting, just one wire to place one foot in front of the other and two wires to support my clenching fists. With my invisible thread of doubt gurgling in my belly, I make my way across and hope that it is the only three-wire swingbridge left on our trek.

The Deception-Mingha route becomes our next obstacle. It is a mountain crossing that gains a reputation because the route follows the Deception River up to 3,500-foot Goat Pass and down the Mingha River on the other side. Trampers must bounce from side to side and sometimes travel in the rivers—highly changeable due to weather—several times. There is a famed Coast-to-Coast race in New Zealand and the Deception-Mingha route is part of the course. Athletes must complete the sixteen-mile passage in three hours; it takes most hikers two days.

At first, we travel easy on the Deception-Mingha track. We occasionally lose our way among the twisted wasteland of stony creek beds, but splashing through the river time and time again with our boots on is liberating. It does not matter that there are goosebumps all the way up to my thighs from the jarring glacial-fed waters; the muscular currents of the Deception River drown out everything and we slowly crawl up the skyward bend of a trail.

As our elevation increases, the scenery changes. Thick and verdant forest carpets the riverbank and we are scrambling up the wet boulders in a full-body—but clumsy—workout.

By the time we reach Goat Pass Hut, we have crossed the Deception River twenty-one times and my knees are convinced they are pestle and mortar.

Twenty-bed Goat Pass Hut is nearly full due to our 6 P.M. Sunday arrival, but we claim our bunks and get to devouring two dehydrated meals and just about everything that is left in our food bags. I have a few honey-roasted peanuts and one tiny peanut butter packet for the morning, while Justin has three scoops of honey left.

There are four other Te Araroa hikers at the hut—Rob, Joss, Serina and Nicolas—but aside from brief introductions, no one has energy left for talking.

"How about this?" I propose to Justin and Kevin. "Whoever wakes first in the morning—no matter the time—should rally and get us moving. I have town food on my mind." The trailhead where we can hitch to Arthur's Pass is less than eight miles away, so I'm fantasizing about a breakfast, complete with eggs, toast and "streaky" bacon, the name Kiwis give to "American" bacon.

"I like the idea," Kevin says. "I'm in."

At 5 A.M., I stir. I lay there thinking about trying to fall back to sleep, but then remember streaky bacon.

I poke the bunk above me, where Justin is sound asleep.

"I think I hear rain," he mumbles.

I ignore him because it is not raining and I know Justin will look for every excuse to stay in bed. I quietly start the process of wadding my sleeping bag into its stuff sack and deflating my pillow.

"Are we really going to do this?" Justin moans.

"Yes," I whisper, as I gently wake Kevin in the bunk across from me. I cannot shake the vision of bacon strips dancing in my head.

We all slowly make our way into the common room, as to not disturb the other bunk mates. However, there are four people sleeping on the floor and dining tables—presumably late-night arrivals. I nudge two of them to tell them our bunks are open if they want to move into the sleeping area. They do.

As we step outside around 6 A.M., my breath crystallizes in the cone of blue-white light streaming from my headlamp. The sun is just starting to bleed into the sky and a layer of cloud sits in the valley below the peaks, like whipped egg whites in a bowl. The fog lifts like a developing Polaroid an hour into our hike, revealing expansive views of the lush Mingha River valley. We tick off the crossings one by one with water so cold, it could shiver my long leg hair loose.

Down in the ravine, a harsh screech cuts through the morning quiet. There are two keas carving playful patterns in the sky. Like the weka, the kea—the world's only alpine parrot—is a thieving bird. In addition to grabbing human food, they've been known to pull the rubber window lining out of car doors and tear holes in tents. The two kea swoop over us in slow orbits, then disappear into the trees.

By 10 A.M., we are sticking our thumbs out for a ride into Arthur's Pass, just a few miles down the road. Hitchhiking is a combination of chance, timing, sympathy and appearances, but we have more luck in New Zealand than we ever did in America on the Appalachian Trail.

The first car that pulls over only has one seat available, so we send Kevin off first. Minutes later, an American couple on holiday swoops us up.

By 10:45 A.M., I am sitting with a full plate of scrambled eggs, toast, sausage, potatoes and streaky bacon, and it is everything I dreamed it would be.

| 12 |

Te Araroa Hiker Bubble
Day 89-97: 145 miles

From the outside, West Harper Hut fits the bill for being constructed in 1953. Standing alone in an open field, the small square hut's corrugated steel roofing is no match for the storm's determination to blow weather through the rusty gaps.

Kevin's backpack is propped against the tin wall and we hear voices as we draw closer to the door.

"Huh, I guess Nicolas and Serena are taking a break here too," I surmise out loud.

Eight Te Araroa hikers—a few whose names I didn't even catch—left from the Mountain House Hostel in Arthur's Pass this morning. Justin, Kevin and I took advantage of every last minute allowed at the hostel, not checking out until 10:03 A.M. The only non-hiker bunkroom mate had a car and offered us a ride, alleviating the task of finding a hitch back to the trailhead.

After the riverbed travel gave way to the forest, we passed three Te Araroa hikers set up for camping in anticipation of the incoming rain. We bid farewell and moved on to catch up to Kevin, who typically moves faster than us.

The first beads of rain nudge us inside West Harper Hut, although we don't shed our own backpacks, knowing we are planning to move on.

When we enter through the door, we see Nicolas blowing up his air mattress. Nicolas is from France and has been hiking with Serina from Canada since the beginning. Until a week ago, they were part of a larger hiking crew with Eef, PJ and Patrick, whom we met a few days earlier. We liked both Serina and Nicolas, but all of us had the hardest time understanding what Nicolas was saying through his heavy French accent.

"You're not seriously staying here for the night, are you?" Justin snaps. The hut's interior was exponentially worse than the exterior.

"Yes," Nicolas asserts between breaths. We understand that word loud and clear.

"I was thinking I would too," Serina says timidly.

I look at the dirt floor and ripped canvas bunks and know no one could pay Justin to consider sleeping in this rat's nest.

"Well, we're moving on. This historic hut gives me the creeps even from the outside," Justin says with a shiver. "Kevin?"

"Oh yeah," Kevin laughs. "I'm game to keep going if you guys are too. I can feel the history falling on my head."

We wish Serina and Nicolas good luck with the haphazard shelter while we prep to brave the elements. It's less than three miles to the next hut, which has to be an improvement from this. Raincoats come out and on and Kevin darts ahead under a plum purple sky.

"We'll see you at the shelter," we yell.

Five minutes later, we hear thunder. It is only the second time in New Zealand that we've experienced thunder, unlike on the Appalachian Trail where thunderstorms were at least a weekly occurrence.

On the fast, flat trail, we pick up our pace through the car wash. A half hour passes and there is still no sign of the shelter.

"Give me the phone and I'll check where we are," Justin shouts through the pouring rain. As I hand it over, lightning flashes followed immediately by a clap of thunder. Justin's eyes bulge. "You keep going as fast as you can and even when you get to the swingbridge, don't wait for me."

I forgot about the swingbridge. It can't be the best idea to cross a metal structure during a thunderstorm.

As I race ahead, I hear Justin yelp.

I turn and see he has fallen, a consequence of trying to bring up our location on the phone app while walking.

"Keep going!" He orders. "Don't stop!"

Eureka! I am never so happy to see a swingbridge. Once across, the sign reads:

HAMILTON HUT – 15 MINUTES

Five minutes later, the forest opens up to the brick-colored wooden building.

We escape the rain under the hut's awning, but count ten pairs of shoes lined outside the door.

"Shit." Justin grunts.

"Don't worry," I comfort him, pointing to the sign.

HAMILTON HUT – SLEEPS 20

Kevin comes outside.

"It's a full hut—with, actually, a bunch of NOBOs—but there are beds left," he assures us. "How about that estimated time on the DOC sign? It is never less than what it says!"

I breathe a sigh of relief and lament the false Department of Conservation times with Kevin.

Inside the walls, warmed by the multiple bodies, we claim two bunks and drape our sodden clothing all around the hut like decorations, adding to the aroma of funk wafting through the air.

We share the hut with seven northbound Te Araroa hikers. Aside from Hannes, whom we met in Top Wairoa Hut in the Richmond Range, we haven't met very many northbounders. If there are fifty to one hundred southbounders who are attempting the trail this year, there are probably only twenty northbounders. Te Araroa Trust writes the trail notes with southbounders in mind. In fact, our veteran Te Araroa friends, Clara and BJ, said deciphering the notes for their northbound hike nearly drove them mad. On the Appalachian Trail, the typical route is northbound, but there is no good reason since there are guidebooks for both directions.

It is perfect timing for us to run into northbounders. There are two Te Araroa "hazard zones" coming up—The Rakaia and Rangitata Rivers. Our trail notes give these general instructions about the first obstacle:

THE RAKAIA IS A LARGE BRAIDED RIVER WITH UNSETTLED SHINGLE BED. EVEN IN LOW FLOW, IT IS NOT POSSIBLE TO SAFELY FORD THIS RIVER ON FOOT. DON'T RISK A FOOT CROSSING. INSTEAD, GO AROUND

THE ROAD IN A VEHICLE. DOING SO WILL NOT
COMPROMISE THE INTEGRITY OF A THROUGH
TRAMP.

We have been gathering information on the Te Araroa
Facebook group about how to approach both rivers from
other hikers. We heard about a few unsuccessfully
attempting to cross the Rakaia. There are a multitude of
channels of different depths and speeds for both rivers, so
it really isn't just one crossing to combat. According to the
locals, there is no passage—there is only swimming. Also
according to the locals, drowning is the New Zealand
death.

We intend to go with the safer bet and hitch the
sixtyish miles around the Rakaia. However, with less than
twenty permanent residents in the village of Lake
Coleridge and only one road that dead ends there,
achieving a ride is a challenge. We heard about the hitch
taking hikers two days to get around, but once again, still
better than imminent death.

The Rakaia crossing is about twenty-five trail miles
from Hamilton Hut. Our plan is to break up those miles
into two days, arriving to the banks of the Rakaia at Lake
Coleridge Lodge, virtually the only business in the village.
A midday arrival will allow us to pick up our resupply box
and increase our chances of scoring a ride.

Still seventy miles away, the second river, the
Rangitata, has been hit or miss for Te Araroa trampers.
Since our fellow hut mates just came from the section and
crossed triumphantly, we value their fresh information.

"Let me show you on the map." A Canadian
northbounder and his girlfriend spread our map on the
large tables as the rain slaps the metal roof, marking the

windows with tears and dripping to the ground.

"You see this dotted line; it is a farm road. Follow it straight to the end where you see a line of pine trees and there will be an electric fence with barbed wire," he advises, as I feverishly write notes. "Cross the fence and enter the riverbed. The first few tributaries will be easy, only up to your shin. Around the seventh or eighth crossing, it gets deep and fast. See my girlfriend, she is short like you," he points to me. "The water was up to her thigh, but it's no problem." I nod my head, feeling less panicked about the whole thing. "There are about four crossings with swift and deep water like that. But it is no problem. You will see a bridge in the distance; that is your aim for the other side."

Armed with a viable plan, we settle in for the night. We give the northbounders useful information for their travel and turn to gear show and tell. Everyone wants to know what the other is carrying and how much it weighs. It is the typical hiker conversation, and one that Justin loves. The difference in our discussion with Te Araroa hikers is that most people measure in grams, not ounces like us.

Knowing we have a shortened day heading toward Lake Coleridge, we stick around until Nicolas and Serina show up at 9 A.M. They inform us that that history—and mice—fell on their heads in West Harper Hut.

At our first river crossing of the day, Kevin zips through and I follow. Justin is still on the other bank, looking up and down the river for a rock hop option. He sits down and starts unlacing his boots.

"What are you doing?" I shriek across the frothing torrent.

"I don't want to get my boots wet."

"This is probably the first crossing of many," I argue. I've come to terms with wet boots.

"You're probably right, but I'm going to chance it."

Each time we lose minutes when Justin removes his socks and boots, it feels like someone turned on the heat for the kettle and I am going to blow. But, by the fourth river, he gives in and leaves his boots on. Today's river crossing count hits twenty-one.

The next day, we travel the metal roads into Lake Coleridge, picking grit out of our eyes every time a car passes. We run into a married Kiwi couple who are walking the South Island. From afar, they appear to be Icelandic warriors, complete with the male wearing a kilt. They are taking photos of every hiker they meet and their final count for 2014-15 turns out to be 147.

At Lake Coleridge Lodge, we catch up to another Te Araroa tramper we met briefly in Arthur's Pass: David from Texas.

David's personality is generally reserved compared with his five-foot-eleven-inch frame and oasis of black fuzz on his face. But, if his matching red shorts and glasses are an indication of what he's really thinking, quirky would be the best word to describe the twenty-something Texan.

At least fifteen packages of ramen spill from David's box.

"I'm so sick of ramen. Lunch and dinner, day after day," he whines. "Do you want some?"

Adding five more dehydrated dinners to our stash—but virtually nothing for breakfast and lunch and definitely a chocolate shortage—our maildrop package is, once again, meager in supplies. We are planning to hitch to Methven, a town with an actual grocery store, today, but we will never turn down free food, so we grab four packages of ramen from David.

"You eat ramen? I thought you were stoveless," I inquire of David.

"I am," he acknowledges. "I don't cook my ramen. I carefully open the package, pour some water in and wait ten minutes. It works better with more time, but it's good enough."

Cold ramen anytime sounds like a surefire way to disgust me, but we eat our oatmeal cold, so I don't judge.

The four of us meander out to the road to try our luck at hitching the long ride into Methven. We run into two British Te Araroa trampers, Rob and Joss. We met them briefly at Goat Pass Hut, but didn't exchange more than a handful of words.

"We have a bloke coming to pick us up at twelve and take us to Christchurch. A contact I have from Hi-Tec, a shoe company that supports my hike," Rob strokes his beard as he explains.

"Hi-Tec? What?" I exclaim. "We've worked with them in the States!"

Justin and I exchange glances and know this is a serendipitous moment and realize we probably just need to name drop to get ourselves a ride with Rob's Hi-Tec liaison. Hi-Tec was one of the sponsors for our *Backpacker* speaking tour. It's at least worth a try, considering we have been in Lake Coleridge village for an hour and have not seen a single car drive by. We hardly give Rob a choice in the matter as we linger the extra few minutes until the white SUV wrapped in Hi-Tec logos pulls up.

A cleancut gentleman exits the vehicle and shakes hands with Rob, eying us dubiously.

"I thought you just had one mate with you," Lance remarks.

Boldly, Justin goes into a spiel trying to yogi a ride for as many of us as possible.

"I can really only fit two of yas, because of the seatbelt law."

Justin and I turn to David and Kevin sympathetically.

"But we can squeeze in the back with the packs," Kevin petitions eagerly.

Lance scratches his head and traces his foot around in the dirt. The four of us nervously pass glances.

"If we get pulled over, you're paying the ticket!" Lance proclaims. "Let's get a move on!"

Lance drops David at Rakaia Gorge campground, us in Methven and Kevin goes with Rob and Joss all the way to Christchurch to pick up his spare pair of trail runners he mailed himself. He hopes to meet back up with us either in Methven or on the trail.

Methven is a single main street town, but complete with a grocery store and a few choices for hostels, so we are satisfied. When the hostel manager at Methven's Mt. Hutt Bunkhouse hands us two towels for showering, we realize we picked a winner. After sharing an eleven-by-fourteen-inch pack towel between the two of us for the past three months, happiness comes in the form of our own full-body towels.

We walk to the post office to mail forward our surplus of dehydrated meals. At the Four Square Supermarket, we supplement the rest of our provisions and run into Ole, our German friend from the North Island.

"De only reason you catch me is because I take days off here because of injury." The trail has not changed Ole.

On the streets of Methven, we bump into Serina and Nicolas, who bemoan the fact that they got to Lake Coleridge as our white Hi-Tec SUV was pulling away.

"Two hours later, we got a ride," Serina growls.

Turns out, there are two other Te Araroa hikers in town, one of which is Dan from Wisconsin. I've seen his name in the hut books, but he had been way ahead of us. He has completed the trail and is on his way back north via Methven.

Through various conversations, the seven of us decide to eat dinner at the Blue Pub, not to be confused with the Brown Pub across the street.

"What's been your favorite and least favorite part of the South Island?" I ask Dan while circling a french fry in my ketchup-mayonnaise concoction.

"I really like the Two Thumbs track, but hated the tussock," he responds, his eyes unflinchingly fixed on my face. I can't place the Two Thumbs track in my mind, but all this tussock talk is starting to give me a facial tick.

As we are leaving the Blue Pub at 7 P.M., Kevin is pulling his backpack out of a stranger's car.

"What are the chances?" I put my arms up, happy he was able to find us so quickly.

"I figured I'd find you guys at the pub," he exclaims.

We tell him about the shuttle to the trailhead we arranged with a school bus at 6 A.M. Kevin is ragged from running all around Christchurch retrieving his shoes and resupplying, but still plans to depart with us, Serina and Nicolas in the morning.

Methven Travel operates the buses for the four area schools. There is one child who lives on the Rakaia River near our Glenrock Stream trailhead, so the bus company decided to capitalize on hiker needs by offering the shuttle. Justin, of course, worked his "deal" magic since there were five of us, so we each paid $20 for the ride. Never in America would they allow dirty, stinky hikers to share a bus ride with schoolchildren.

Given our 7:30 A.M. arrival to the trailhead, the five of us walk through a wispy veil of fog floating upward, revealing a sun-bleached landscape ahead. Nicolas and Serina count on staying just a few miles in, so we say our goodbyes once again.

Nowhere in New Zealand are the landscape contrasts so abrupt and apparent than in the transition from the wet forests in the west to the semi-arid mountains and plains of the east. Thanks to the prevailing westerly winds hitting the barrier of the Southern Alps and dropping enormous quantities of rain and snow on the west, the east ends up with blowing dry, hot air.

During our next few days, we walk on an Earth hardened into a crust from sun where scree slopes and tussock grasslands mingle, with catacomb cold rivers blasting through the valleys below.

Most of our first day is spent crossing the Ashburton River and Round Hill Creek—fifty-four crossings, actually. The hypothermia-inducing waterways never rise above our shins, but it is exhausting, both physically and mentally.

Tussock, the word I had been hearing for the last ninety-two days, finally comes to life for me. The eastern hills, too dry to support forest, instead grow five types of tussock and I see a huge spread in front of us. The scene is beautiful with their golden blond-highlighted tips shaking and rustling from side to side like pom poms. This serenity is a fleeting moment.

Following not one iota of a trail, Justin uses the monocular to decide the general direction of travel. What I realize is that walking through tussock reminds me of the fun house rides from my youth. Similar to walking on the uneven planks in the fun house, travel through tussock has me desperately trying to find food placements among the narrow gaps between roots.

Meanwhile, there is an explosion of long, willowy blades, slimmer than a reed of grass that tries to trip and strangle me. A game of hide and seek ensues as the bigger, six-foot high clumps obscure Justin and Kevin ahead and I have to hoot to them to assure I am traveling the right direction. The whole underfoot appears to be lathered in slick oil, as a bonus.

"I don't think there are any other places in this world where the plant life is deadlier than the wildlife," I bark.

We climb well past the point where our bodies are screaming from exhaustion. Kevin is waiting for us at the top of the saddle in a reprieve from the tussock.

"I'm going to keep pushing to Double Hut. I think it's only another three or four miles," he reports. Kevin does not love his tent, unlike us. We've slept in our Big Agnes Copper Spur tent well over 150 nights and Justin much prefers it next to shelters. Plus, we are warned that the huts in this section are a bit tired, with build dates like 1890.

"We're spent, so go on. We'll find a spot to set up our tent among the tussock," Justin responds. "Hopefully we'll catch up with you tomorrow."

Shortly thereafter, we find a prime chunk of land to place our tent—a little exposed to the elements—but the weather seems clear. Our 360-degree view is an endless line of camel humps, all barren of vegetation. As the evening casts its chilly shadows, we retreat to the tent.

Around 9 P.M., the winds are stirring up a magic potion and we have to close our rainfly doors because dirt is blowing inside. *Whap, whap, whap.* There is little sleep. Instead, there is wind.

The few miles to Kevin's hut is an impossibly overgrown hill filled not only with tussock, but with pokey plants.

Matagouri and speargrass, or "spiky Spaniard"—which sounds like it should be an exotic drink—are both spiny colonizers of dry places on the South Island. The Maori people have used the thorns of the matagouri bushes for tattoos, so it makes sense that walking through them feels like an inexperienced nurse trying to give an intravenous injection. The Spaniard grass have dozens of rigid spikes and footlong leaves that look flax, but are solid and taper to a needlepoint. As we stride through, the plants attack us like sticky toddlers. My ankle-high gaiters help some, but I wish I had the knee-high gaiters the Kiwis recommend. War wounds are cool though.

After the wrestling match with the plant life, the track gets fast and easy on widening flats. At the junction for Double Hut, there is no sign of Kevin. We can see the hut, and I am curious about it. In 1951, Sir Edmund Hillary, the first person to summit and descend safely from Mount Everest, stayed in the hut during a training climb and signed the wall in pencil. Hillary is a national hero in New Zealand, but the hut is a good quarter of a mile away, so we skip seeing his autograph.

We assume Kevin is in front of us, as our unexpectedly

slow progress has put us at 9:45 A.M. already.

Though we woke to near-freezing temperatures, thermal oppression occurs within the hour in the sun-drenched, treeless valley we walk. We protect ourselves with sunscreen, but no matter; our skin has been baked a deep, terracotta brown and resembles leather from three months of exposure.

After nearly twenty-four miles, we camp just four miles from the Rangitata River without Kevin and next to a dried-up lake. We can see our obstacle and all its braids fanned out like branchy fingers in the distance; the Rangitata looks about as friendly as a tornado.

The next morning, Kevin is waiting for us at the carpark across from the Rangitata.

We follow the advice of the Canadian hut mate and head for the distinct line of pine trees on the horizon. Only I am zapped by the electric fence, but I am the shortest.

Next, it is all riverbed rock travel. I can barely see the other side of the river, but the high peaks appear tantalizingly nearby. Insides curled tight, my anxiety and adrenaline threaten to overwhelm once again. I try to control it, focusing instead on the stony escarpments hurting my feet and the fact that at least fifty other trampers have forded successfully in just the last month.

We come to the first barricade of whooshing water. It is as clear as saran wrap down to the rockbed and is about six feet across. Kevin steps in first and slowly moves to the other side.

"You saw. Only ankle deep. Good footing."

Justin and I bound through, and though the water sends ice through my veins, it is easy peasy.

We cross ten more tributaries like the first. My heart

rate has finally normalized just as we come to a larger braid. It is at least two car lengths to the other side. We can hardly hear each other over the booming surge. We walk up and down the bank, scouting the best passage. The cascades look as thick as syrup, with silver at its fringes, prompting almost a hallucinatory quality.

I step in at the same time as Justin, who stays close by. Poles first planted for maximum stability, I can feel them reverberating. With a healthy mix of ignorance and insanity as the water laps above my knees, I plod through slowly. I shove my right foot into the rocky underfoot and wait a moment to do the same with the other foot. I am staring down at my feet until I notice the embankment. Kevin puts his hand out to help me up. On dry ground, I exhale.

"I have to poop," Justin announces. His irregular bowel movements are especially intensified after a town stop. The high-caloric, high-fat burger, topped with New Zealand's specialty of fried egg and beets—plus fries—from Methven's Blue Pub is gurgling and churning inside his belly and diving for its escape hatch. It is never an opportune time or place, but this takes the cake. The parched rocky landscape is about to be fertilized.

"Good luck digging a hole here!" I laugh. "At least there are tons of rocks for wiping!"

Kevin and I forge ahead to give Justin a semblance of privacy. Droplets dance on the river and I look at the threatening clouds in the distance over Mount Sunday, also known as Edoras in *The Lord of the Rings*. We are at crossing number twelve of at least fifteen, so I take solace that we are past the halfway mark.

Justin catches back up and we successfully ford a few

other sketchy braids of the Rangitata.

Finally, we reach the road. Six miles and seventeen crossings in two hours and twenty minutes. Shoes and socks off, we take a well-deserved lunch break at the Bush Stream carpark, the trailhead that will take us into the Two Thumb track.

I give silent credit to Dan, who we met in Methven and who praised the Two Thumb track. I instantly understand his accolades. The high-country trail takes us thirty-five miles across a landscape that easily eulogizes about the empty mountain spaces and untamed wilderness of New Zealand. During our three days, the sun pokes out shyly in between wispy clouds, making the temperature perfect for walking. Every night, the full moon hangs like a stage prop against a black curtain. It is in this stretch we also reach the highest point of Te Araroa, Stag Saddle, at approximately 6,300 feet.

The huts continue to be disheveled from decades of use by sheep musterers. The shelters were built for crews gathering merino sheep in the mountains, thus not meant to impress trampers.

This is also one of the designated areas for hunting tahr, native to the Himalayas, and chamois, a European goat-antelope—both introduced in the 1900s for sport. As a result, the huts are full of young men out for a kill. Justin and I camp outside the huts two of the nights, but we are drawn to the eight-bunk Royal Hut.

In 1970, twenty-one-year-old Prince Charles and nineteen-year-old Princess Anne flew in via helicopter to check out the musterers' shelter on Mesopotamia Station, one of New Zealand's best-known, high-alpine farms. The royal party had tea and explored a little bit, but left just as quickly as they arrived. Their impression, however, was long-lasting, as the Department of Conservation renamed the hut to be Royal Hut.

Royal Hut is the nicest bunkhouse we've seen in awhile but we are being generous given its poorly insulated, corrugated sheet metal walls, leaky roof and part-dirt, part-concrete floor. I wonder what Prince Charles would think now.

For us, we thought it would be a good place to do something we haven't done the entire trek—stop early.

While we were in Wellington, we rented *The Hobbit* on our iPad from iTunes, thinking it would be good to have a source of entertainment while we waited out weather in the South Island huts. Given our stroke of luck with Mother Nature, it has been unnecessary. Now, our thirty-day rental is about to expire, so the three of us decide to hunker down in perfectly clear weather and enjoy *The Hobbit* on 7.9 inches of screen space.

Two young northbound section hikers, Johannes and Tom, as well as our fellow Te Araroa southbound walker, David, join us at Royal Hut. They lay in their respective bunks watching the movie with only their ears.

Near the end of the Two Thumb Track, we start seeing views of Lake Tekapo and the sugar-coated mountains of Mount Aspiring National Park. We plan a near-zero day in Tekapo. Carole from Wellington put us in touch with her friends, Caroll and Craig, who own several businesses in Lake Tekapo. They have arranged for us to rent one of their holiday homes at a discounted rate of $100 for the two of us. It is an entire house with a kitchen, showers, laundry and Internet, all to ourselves. We are planning to take a zero day in Queenstown for the Hiker Trash Party on Saint

Patrick's Day, otherwise this would have been the place to do it.

Once in town, we are thankful for the prearranged housing situation. It is mayhem with tourists enjoying their Chinese New Year holiday in the tiny village that is only one mile in perimeter. Kevin has to go to all three hostels in Lake Tekapo before he scores just about the last bunk.

Along with David, the three of us eat at McKenzie's Café. Their cinnamon rolls—particularly the cream cheese caramel one—will go down in history for Justin and Kevin. To this day, they still hail its existence.

We pick up a big feast of frozen pizzas and a half gallon of Tip Top Boysenberry Ripple Ice Cream at the Four Square, and invite Kevin over for dinner and unlimited Internet. The word "unlimited Internet" is extremely rare in New Zealand. Typically, we have bandwidth the size of a pinkie and speed like a turtle, so this is a major bonus. The three of us say hardly three words to each other as we bury our heads close to our devices, soaking it all up.

| 13 |

Book of Questions
Days 98-104: 117.6 miles

ALTHOUGH THIS IS "ROAD" WALKING, IT IS A METAL
ROAD THROUGH SPECTACULAR SCENARY AND
YOU'RE UNLIKELY TO SEE A VEHICLE ALL DAY.

We take comfort in the trail notes regarding the next
sixty-five miles. Except that within an hour, we are up to a
count of seven cars, all of which shoot gravel every which
way like a fistful of jacks.

We haven't seen trees in at least two weeks and I
suspect it is three hundred degrees. We all need a break
and collapse into a single patch of shade.

"I'm hot." I say as I inch away from Justin, whose body
heat is radiating into my space. I look at my thermometer
keychain and even in the shade, the mercury is up to the
high eighties. I munch on a Bumper Bar and wish I had
New Zealand's signative frozen Sprite from McDonald's to
get rid of the cotton balls in my mouth. The air is so thick

I am chewing it. Glimpses of Lake Pukaki's crystal waters tantalize us. It is our hundredth day on the trail and I am irritated.

Things finally get exciting as nature's most vivid palette reveals a cloudless blue sky pierced by the gleaming white dominance of Mount Cook, the tallest mountain in New Zealand at 12,218 feet. At the mountain's pure white base, Lake Pukaki blends brilliantly with the feathery toi toi fringing the lake's edge to give yet another contrast of color. Lake Pukaki is otherworldly. Fed by nearby Tasman and Hooker glaciers in Mount Cook National Park and impacted by rock flour—glacier rock particles finely grounded in the alpine catchments—it presents in an iridescent turquoise color.

Claiming another epic camping spot, we set up meal time on the shoreline of Lake Pukaki and eat our Beef Vegetable Stew dehydrated meal with a side of Mount Cook. In a country that is still happily free of serious air pollution, the clarity and flamingo-colored alpenglow the setting sunlit angle strikes on the crest of Mount Cook is like a theatrical spotlight. It is memories like this that are burned in my imagination forever.

Our roadwalk gives way the next day to the well-graded and level Alps 2 Ocean Cycle Trail following around Lake Pukaki. Some Te Araroa hikers have even chosen to trade in their backpacks and poles for bikes and helmets in this sixty-mile section of the trail.

Kevin suggests playing "Book of Questions" to cope with the doldrums of flat walking. He has a PDF on his phone with more than two hundred questions about our values, beliefs, love, money, generosity, pride and life in general.

It is so easy to create deep connections and life-long friendships on the trail. You are among like-minded people who get it. You spend a lot of time together. You even know each other's bowel movement habits.

It has been nice to add a third musketeer to our party for the past twenty days. Even though Justin and I don't fight often, I've noticed petty irritations amplifying into intolerable aggravations. The inescapable intimacy of a twenty-nine-square-foot tent is enough to fray anyone's nerves. Kevin and I have similar personalities—with our eternal optimism, natural collaborator, non-confrontational, peacekeeper ways—so I feel like I have an extra ally when there are disagreements.

The situation with Kevin seems familiar to us. On our Appalachian Trail thru hike, we met a young guy, Mac, or "Fire Marshall," our first day at the summit of Mount Katadhin. Night after night, we ended up at the same shelter or campsite together. We didn't even know Mac's last name, but by the time we finished the first two hundred miles, it was clear we were a team of three. We ended up finishing together and are great friends still today.

"Would you accept $1 million to leave the country and never set foot in it again?" Kevin starts.

"Without a doubt," Justin blurts almost immediately. "I've seen enough of America."

"Can other people come see me?" I ask.

"I guess you could interpret the question however you want," Kevin says.

"No," I respond. "It would be too hard to leave everyone altogether and my family probably couldn't visit wherever I am."

"I'm with you, Patrice," Kevin says. "$1 million wouldn't do it, but $10 million might. It has to be enough that I can afford to transport my family and friends to wherever I am whenever I want."

"I would do it for $10 million, too," I admit.

A year ago, we didn't even know Kevin existed. But now we are walking a trail together, about to share deep, dark secrets. This is the story of trail friendships you can't make up.

"Okay, next question," Kevin announces. "Would you rather die peacefully among friends at age 50, or painfully and alone at age 80? Assume that most of the last 30 years would be good ones."

"I think being alone would be very tough," Justin reflects. "I would rather have the comfort of my family and friends around me talking about all the good times we had and telling stories."

"Yeah, I have no desire to live to 80, alone or not alone," I state.

"Okay, wow, I'm the complete opposite," Kevin claims. "Painfully and alone at 80. A death would have to be unfathomably shitty to overwhelm an extra thirty years of good life."

A few cyclists whiz past us.

Kevin continues, "I wouldn't mind outliving my family and friends, assuming they had a good run and didn't die early, and would have no problems ending my own pain when the time came."

"I have to pee," I report. "Let me duck into these trees and I'll catch up."

When I catch up to the guys, they are still talking about dying young versus living long.

"Alright, we'll move on from that depressing topic." Kevin reads, "What would constitute a perfect evening for you?"

"I could probably guess Justin's. It most certainly has something to do with music," I could almost hear Justin's mind at work daydreaming the perfect scenario.

"Yep. A concert with my favorite bands—From Good Homes, Railroad Earth, String Cheese Incident and The Grateful Dead. Catered food and craft beer. A backdrop of mountains and lake in front of it. All my friends and family around me dancing. Ending the night sleeping under the stars in a tent with my love."

"You get brownie points for the last part," I smile.

The day flies by thanks to our introspective conversations. We can see the drive-in Pines Camping Area—our goal for the day—in the distance.

"Okay, last one for today. If there were only three days left, what would you do?"

"Easy for me. I would seriously go back and rent that house in Lake Tekapo, and utilize their unlimited Internet to FaceTime and Skype everyone I can with last conversations. All the while, I'd soak up the incredible views of the lake and be thankful for a life well lived."

Even though it is only 3:30 P.M., we stop after eighteen miles. Kevin had been talking about taking a side trip to Mt. Cook National Park, and we are near the access road to the park on the other side of the lake.

"I think I'm going to try to hitch there tonight. I'll explore the park and catch up to you in a few days," he reasons. "I figure, why not?"

We say our goodbyes once again, knowing he will have no problem catching us.

Justin and I set up camp among the pine trees, then walk out to a clearing for our dining with a view. To the north, a churning plume of spindrift spills off Mount Cook's summit as we watch the dramatic cloud formations and sunset over the lake.

"Weather is definitely coming in," I comment. "Hopefully Kevin doesn't get caught in it tomorrow."

The placid lake turns viscous overnight, whipped up by the overhead storm. The patchwork of whitecaps on the lake, rapidly dropping temperatures and shrouded Mount Cook tells us we are in for a crappy hike. We have less than eight miles to get to Twizel, where we plan to resupply and move on.

Morale sinks way down in the gutter as the weather continues to turn sinister. Rain and hail stalk us the entire way into town. The wind is flapping hard against my waterproofs as if I were skydiving. I wipe the river of mucus from my nose with my wet rain jacket sleeve. There isn't a place on my body where the singing cold hasn't gripped. I put one foot in front of the other and hope that there is a hot chocolate waiting for me in Twizel. Wasn't it just yesterday that I was dying of heat? Now I'm turning hypothermic.

We hit the outskirts of Twizel and try desperately to get our sense of direction for the grocery store. A few turns and I see a sign for "High Country Backpackers."

I stop and turn to Justin and hope he can see my sad eyes under my hood.

"I think I want to stay," I sniffle.

He doesn't object. We make our way to the office doors.

"Hi," Justin says. "Do you have any bunks for tonight?"

"Fresh out," says the man behind the desk. "Thare's a youth camp here taking over the hostel. Only thing I have is a hotel room."

"How much is that?"

"One hundred and fifteen."

Justin turns to me and rolls his eyes.

"I can't," I sputter. "I just can't. I need to warm up."

I take a twenty-minute shower before I feel my body temperature rise back to normal.

In between raindrops, we run over to the Four Square for a gluttonous resupply. In the chocolate aisle, we run into Kevin.

"The weather was wild at the park. There were only four of us crazy enough to be at the campground. There's a community kitchen and we all slept inside it."

We convince Kevin to stay and try room stacking since we have a second bed, but run into the manager on our way back.

"How much to add our buddy to our room?" Justin asks, as if we had been looking for him.

"Thirty dollars." We turn to Kevin.

"Why not?" Kevin shrugs his shoulders.

The three of us cram into our overpriced hotel room and get to sorting food and updating blogs.

"Kev, we've decided you have earned a trail name," I smile. This is Kevin's first hike over one hundred miles, warranting the tradition of a trail name. "Why Not!"

"I like it," he nods his head. "Fitting."

An hour later, I look up from my phone to the window. "Shit," I blurt.

Justin and Kevin react as I point outside. The skies are clearing and it's still early enough in the day to get some miles in.

"That sucks," Justin agrees. "Too bad we've already committed."

The weather remains mostly clear the rest of the afternoon, but we wake to pouring rain. The forecast shows rain through 1 P.M. We take advantage of our 10 A.M. checkout time and head to the bakery to wait out the rain some more.

Serina, Nicolas and David all walk in, drenched to the bone.

"I really need a shower," Serina jabbers.

"Damn, we just checked out from our room!" I apologize.

"How did you get a room?" Serina asks. "I heard there are no rooms available. We even checked at the campground and there is no room."

"I guess we were lucky, but we paid a fortune!" I reassure her.

By 11 A.M., there had been an entire thirty minutes of no rain, so Justin, Kevin and I decide to take our chances and go, leaving Serina, Nicolas and David to hope for a spot to open at the Holiday Park.

"This is fun!"

"It's," David hesitates, "something."

I keep my rain shell on as we leave town, hoping that will ward off the weather.

Kevin fires up the PDF on his phone for more Book of Questions.

"Whom do you admire most?"

"Go ahead, you answer first for a change, Kev," I say.

"Elon Musk."

"Who?" Justin and I blurt simultaneously.

"He's an autodidactic polymath who takes a big picture approach to defining humanity's most pressing problems and then sets about solving them," Kevin takes a breath. "The Mars mission is an inspiring goal and the portfolio of companies that he has had a hand in creating to address the challenges of that undertaking—SpaceX, Tesla, Solar City—is seriously impressive. His choice to focus on the biggest risks to our species is incredibly admirable and his ability to take massive, concrete steps toward developing the technologies necessary to mitigate those risks is even more so."

Kevin has multiple degrees, including a master's in international affairs, and has worked as an accountant and practiced law, so it doesn't surprise me that half of what he's said has gone over our heads.

"My answer is way more basic. I admire my mom. She is the most selfless person I know and she never feels judged or jealous. I aspire to be more like her."

"Mine is simple too," Justin says. "I've always admired my Uncle Pete for his kindness, sense of humor and free spirit. But he also took care of both my grandma and grandpa until they died and that's a really tough thing to do."

We start a short uphill, so we all take a momentary breather from talking.

Justin continues at the crest, "but I also have a second person I admire and this is going to surprise you, babe."

I cock my head.

"I admire Janice." Janice is my sister.

"She works so hard—professionally and at home as a mother. She has so much shit to deal with in her home life, but she always has a smile on her face and I've never seen her complain."

"That is so sweet, Justin," I say, squeezing back a tear. He is right. My sister has two children and while I love my niece and nephew wholeheartedly, they are a handful. Janice works full-time, does the majority of the parenting and is almost as selfless as my mom.

"Okay, this is more lighthearted and interesting," Kevin remarks. "If you could have free, unlimited service for five years from an extremely good cook, chauffeur, housekeeper, masseuse or personal secretary, which would you choose?"

"Cook." Justin announces. "I've always wished I learned how to cook well. But I'm too cheap to buy really good ingredients. A cook would solve that. Smoothies everyday!" Justin and I both like to cook, but he is right. We could certainly up our game to more gourmet cooking. There are some days, though, I wish Justin had a secretary. Ever since we started sharing work roles—including a cell phone and an e-mail—my communication duties have doubled as I often play Justin's personal assistant.

"I think masseuse would be my answer," I offer. "But I like them all."

"For me, it's a hard choice between the chef and secretary. Gonna have to go with secretary. I hate dealing with administrative BS and like to cook, so I'd probably do some of that even if I had a chef. Certainly wouldn't mind having someone do my travel planning and logistical work for me."

"Yeah, I'm sure you have had to do some major logistical planning for all your hikes," I sympathize, thinking about the logistics I arranged just for this trail alone. "All while traveling. Yikes!"

"You guys want to pull off for a snack and break?" Justin asks. "I gotta go to the bathroom and see a sheltered area by the lake for us to sit."

We were now walking along Lake Oahu, which is smaller than Lake Pukaki, but just as pretty. The skies look threatening, but it's still not raining. I dare not tempt the weather gods and keep my rain gear on. I pull out our jar of Nutella and graham crackers. I added peanut butter to the nutella container back in town and I'm pretty certain I found a new favorite trail snack.

Following a fifteen-minute break, we jump back on the cycle path for the rest of the day.

"Alright, here's an interesting one," Kevin declares. "Since adolescence, in what three-year period do you feel you experienced the most personal growth and change?"

We all give it some silent thought.

"I can go first," I pipe up. "I moved clear across the country after college to participate in a post-graduation volunteer program, and that period on my own— thousands of miles from my friends and family—in my early twenties, without a doubt, shaped who I am. It was a learning and growing experience."

"I would say for me, it was my last few years of college," Justin chimes in.

"For my first two years of college, I didn't know what direction I wanted to go, so I majored in business and partying. One day, I noticed a sign about an internship at Disney World. I met with a professor about it and she introduced the idea of majoring in recreation. Our talks excited me. I realized I didn't need to sit behind a desk and work nine to five in an office. I knew I loved being outside, camping, hiking and being with people. I had no idea this could be a career and I could find atypical jobs."

I am surprised at how many things I am learning about my own husband. I knew he started as a business major in college, but didn't realize how formative those years were. Sometimes I wish he would talk more about his Crohn's, as I only know what I've researched about the disease. I am certain having a chronic illness shapes a person, but maybe it hasn't fully done that for him yet.

"I eventually changed my major, applied for this Disney internship and scored it. The Disney College Program taught me more than college did and molded me into the recreation professional I am today."

A few bikers slow to a stop alongside us and ask what we're doing. Kevin lets us tell them we've come all the way from Cape Reinga. As usual, their mouths drop and they bid us "good an yas."

"Okay, I don't think this question applies to any of us, but when was the last time you stole something?"

"Actually," I interject, "I stole something in Twizel!"

"What?" Justin and Kevin turn to look at me and I feel like my words hit like a neatly thrown grenade.

"I went to get a butter packet for my bagel and they had them all lined up alongside jellies and peanut butters. I grabbed the butter, but as I was turning away, noticed the sign said $0.50 per packet!" I plead, "I know, minus ten points for me, but no one was around, so I justified that one stolen packet was not going to be missed!"

Kevin smirks and Justin says, "tsk, tsk, tsk" while shaking his finger.

"Oooh, here's a revealing one," Kevin announces. "What are your most compulsive habits?"

Kevin's voice breaks the silence. "I can go first on this

one because I am fully willing to admit I check Twitter first thing in the morning when I'm off trail, I get pissed off by Republican political machinations and I eat too many dehydrated mangoes."

I laugh. "Those are interesting, especially in combination." I sigh. "I know Justin would love to answer this for me, but I am also willing to admit I frequently talk and interrupt people." Justin is nodding his head. "Not on purpose. I mean well, I care about what other people have to say. I never realized I was doing it until a friend pointed it out in 2010. Ever since then, I've been trying to work on it, but it annoys the heck out of Justin." He stays silent, but I know he could lecture me on this trait. "I realized my mom and sister also do it, too, so I guess it is an ingrained habit."

"Justin? What about yours?" Kevin pries.

"Um, hmm, I don't know." He turns to me. "Babe, what about me? What are my bad habits?"

Oh boy. Is this my chance to air my grievances about him? I could say he is so indecisive and it feeds negatively into my indecisiveness. That sometimes he is harshly judgmental when he first meets someone, especially when it comes to gear choices and hikers on this trail. That he is easily distracted and manages his time poorly. That sometimes he sweats the small stuff—like spilled water on his favorite magazine—a little too much. That sometimes he comes across condescending and passive aggressive when he talks.

Instead, I snort and stammer, "I don't know, I think the question is for you to answer yourself," looking off into the distance.

"Um maybe it's that I don't let go of control and

delegate tasks to others," he finally says. "It's hard to say to someone else, 'you can do this or that,' because I usually have an opinion about how it's done."

Well, that's one way to say he's a little too passionate and can be opinionated. It is just as well to leave snakes under rocks because pointing out someone's faults is about as effective as telling someone to quit smoking.

The three of us find another sleepy hamlet for the night under the trees with Lake Oahu as our dining room. The surrounding mountains are looming menacingly like a prehistoric monster, some with their mantle of winter snow, as the mountains of Mount Aspiring National Park get closer and closer.

The next day, we head up from the road leaving the lake views behind, first on a mountain bike trail through the bush. The shades of green are short-lived though as the undulating hills turn back to their russet potato color speckled by tussock and speargrass. The trail notes are concerning:

THIS TRACK PROVIDES A GOOD TRANSITIONAL TRAMP FOR MODERATELY EXPERIENCED TRAMPERS LOOKING TO GO THE NEXT STEP, OFF THE HEAVILY USED AND WELL-GROOMED TRACKS WHERE THEY LEARNED THEIR CRAFT AND ONTO TE ARAROA'S MORE REMOTE AND DEMANDING SECTIONS.

Where in the heck were these well-groomed tracks they speak of? My memory is etched with more remote and demanding sections than well-groomed. And now that we are well past the halfway point of the trail, I do not have any interest in taking it to the next level.

Down in the valley, the grass is swampy and we negotiate endless small streams, but no matter, we have to cross the Ahuriri River today, described as "the largest unbridged flow along Te Araroa's South Island route." The rumor is that this year, Ahuriri's single braid is worse than the Rangitata as a whole.

We climb up the small hill for our first glimpse of the river in the Ahuriri Valley below us. Still a half mile from the river bank, all we see is a deceptively benign ribbon of blue contrasted against a brown and grey canvas. On the other side of the Ahuriri, the cliffs look like they were chopped from the Earth with an axe. The other side is our goal for a camp spot tonight. It is already 5 P.M. and climbing the steep rock after nearly twenty miles of walking for the day is not a task any of us desire.

The three of us stand on that hill for ten minutes or so, quietly discerning the best way to ford the river from up above.

Kevin breaks the silence by asking "Where did others say they crossed?"

I give my full report of how most people went downstream and found a belly-button deep crossing that was safe. We all nod in silent agreement. Justin alternates between looking at the map and the river. I look over his shoulder and read the trail notes, which merely suggest finding "the most practical route."

"Well, we survived the Rangitata, and fifty million other crossings, so this can't be much worse," Justin says as he bounds down the hill.

As we reach the banks, I get a gut punch of panic for yet another dangerous river crossing. The Ahuriri is moving about as fast as a bicycle going downhill. It looked a whole lot less intimidating from up above. I cannot see the bottom of this river. The calcium from the surrounding quartz-ridden bluffs has left the river silty and looking cloudy, hiding all the eddies and its depth. The good news is we find a spot that is only twenty feet across.

"I think we should take off our pants," I suggest. "I know it sounds weird, but it's the end of the day and I have no interest in putting on wet pants tomorrow morning. It's bad enough we'll have to put on our wet shoes." Justin and Kevin nod their head without taking their eyes off the river.

As we are derobing our pants and loosening our backpacks, Justin instructs loudly over the river.

"Let's link arms and put Patrice in the middle. If you feel unsafe at all, babe, you make the call to go back."

I shiver—maybe because of the cold, but probably because of the anticipation of crossing the Ahuriri.

"Ready?" Justin says as he grabs my tense left arm. I hook my right arm with Kevin's and we all angle upstream. At ankle deep, the cold water takes my breath away. At thigh deep, a river-icicle knifes into my bones. The water stays at this level and swirls around us effortlessly.

"You okay?" Justin checks in. I shake my head yes.

The water reaches my navel and I lift my shoulders and chest, as I would in yoga class, to stand taller. We are about halfway across the river. I see Kevin's single trekking pole vibrating like a guitar string.

Kevin's foot slips on a rock and I tighten my arm muscles to brace him. He lets out a sigh of relief when he manages to catch his balance.

On the other side, we quickly use the short stubby trees as drying racks for our shirts, socks and shoes, setting up our own laundromat. The area is pockmarked with rabbit poop and holes, but I am distracted by the fact we have survived yet another river in New Zealand.

A vast blanket of white hangs in the valley the next morning. Through the haze, we scour the cliff for our path and finally see an orange pole. We scuttle up the impossibly steep and crumbly rock. On the plateau above the river, there is maze of animal pads. On the map, it looks like we are meant to navigate the farmland for a mile along the riverbank to find the road and carpark for our next trailhead. Looking around, I see nothing but a ghost-grey veil.

"I've got to use the bathroom," Kevin announces as Justin and I are pulling out our map and notes for the third time today. "I'll catch up."

Through the cloud deck, Kevin becomes nothing more than a silhouette.

I fire up the iHikeGPS NZ app on my phone.

"Um, I think we have to turn right here to get to the road!" I declare. Sure enough, we turn and reach the gravel road and the carpark directly across that will lead us into the Ahuriri Conservation Park.

The park's landscape is beautiful, especially with the low-lying fog hovering over the horseshoe bends of the river. We rise up above the valley and down into it over and over all morning long.

Justin and I both take a bathroom break. From my tree outhouse, I spot the biggest deer I've ever seen in the faraway hills, then another and another.

When Justin and I reunite, he pulls out his monocular to get a closer look.

"I'm pretty sure it's an elk!" he whispers excitedly.

Within minutes, we hear the elk bulgling and rutting. I knew New Zealand farmed elk, but I never thought we'd see them.

After six miles, we stop for lunch at an unnamed hut, thinking Kevin should have caught us by now. We leave a note in the Intentions Book, stating the time we lunched to let him know how far ahead we are.

Up to Martha's Saddle, we follow a bulldozed track with switchbacks. It is odd to see our path scraped down to bedrock by a man-made machine. There must have been a reason the Department of Conservation laid out the path for more than just the trampers, but it remains a mystery and a blessing. At the top, a cold wind bites my cheeks and nose and I turn to avoid it.

"Still no sign of Kevin," I remark, gazing across the valley behind us.

Down the other side, we are sidling loose rock on a path reduced to two feet in width. I prep for the Earth to be ripped out from under me at any moment, while Justin trots along like it's a concrete sidewalk. I pick my way down, down, down to Top Timaru Hut. We both expect to see Kevin at the shelter, thinking he leapfrogged us somehow. But it is empty.

Just as the fading sunlight peeks one last time through the dirty hut windows, lifting dust into the air and drifting it above me, Kevin walks through the door.

"After you guys left me to do my business on the farmland, I got completely turned around," he recants, grinning. "When I finally found the road, I must have walked two or three miles out of my way trying to find the carpark."

The trail undulates in and out of the milky white Timaru River about a dozen times via the forest. Kevin is so frustrated with the repetition that he decides to just walk through the river.

"Why not?" he smirks.

"Don't get lost!" Justin cautions.

We all plan to break at Stody's Hut, promising to leave notes on each other's whereabouts.

Surprisingly, our sidling and undulating takes less time than Kevin's river travel.

The Department of Conservation sign reads:

PAKITUHI HUT 4.5 HOURS

Even though it's already 3:30 P.M., we all agree to push on, though Justin tells us he'll catch up because he has to dig a hole.

"Would you recommend this trail to others?" Kevin pants, as we are lumbering our way straight uphill.

I think long and hard.

"Yes," I finally answer. "I know it's not the most perfect trail and it could use a few switchbacks," I say pointing down, "but in the grand scheme of things, I would suggest it to certain people with some major caveats." I pause to control my wheezing. "Particularly for my seasoned backpacker friends, I would tell them if they've done all the long-distance trails in America—and have an interest in seeing a good majority of New Zealand the adventurous way—they definitely need to add this to their list."

"I don't think I'd advise anyone to do it," he objects. "But part of that is I just don't think I am cut out to be a long-distance hiker. I'll stick to my hundred-mile stints! The other part is it misses some of the most beautiful parts of New Zealand."

"Oh, see, I think it encompasses New Zealand really well. When the Trust designed the trail, they purposely kept it away from the touristy spots. I agree the Great Walks are showcased for a reason, but I don't want to be among the masses," I assert. After another lull to slow my heart palpitations, I add, "If this is your first thru hike, I would never recommend this one. Yet, we met people like Marilyne and Matteo on their first thru hike and they're taking this thing by its horns."

"Yeah, I can't imagine this being your first run at a thru hike!" Kevin snorts.

"Our veteran TA friends advised us to do the North Island differently—like hitching portions, or renting a bike—and we were stubborn and wanted to do the whole darn thing, of course. But, I'd do the same thing— encourage people to hopscotch around the semi-connected dots of worthy tracks."

Through my harmonica breathing, I continue, "One more soap box statement. Not every thru hike is about the physical trail and scenery. Trails build character—not in a single a-ha moment, but over time. When you're out here with your thoughts, day in and day out, and time is like a stagnant river, there's some serious introspection. So for me, this was more about the personal journey and test," I sigh. "This thru hike—or any long-distance hike—is certainly not for everyone. But I stand by the argument that it is a great way to experience Kiwi culture."

We stop for another break at the top of Breast Hill and our arduous workout is rewarded with views of the brochure-blue Lake Hawea. The 9,951-foot alpine horn of Mt. Aspiring shows itself in the distance. It may not have lived up to the trail notes warning of stepping it up a notch, but I silently decide this section's miles should be measured vertically, not horizontally.

"And this," I emphasize, as I turn a slow circle 360 degrees. "New Zealand's untouched wilderness is the main reason I would suggest it."

| 14 |

Tourist Traps
Days 105-113: 117.6

"How much food do you have left?" I ask Kevin.

"One serving of cous cous, a few bites of salami and a few banana chips. What about you guys?"

"About the same. Not nearly enough. Thank God for this café."

We are eating breakfast at a small shop in Lake Hawea and I pull out our maps.

"It's only another fifteen miles to Wanaka. Do you think we can make it?" We've already hiked six miles, and it seems like it will be mostly flat into Wanaka. I could go for real food for dinner. From here until the end, we won't have to go more than four days between resupplies. This whole town-to-town walking comes at a good time. We need the calories. We both weighed ourselves in Lake Tekapo and I dropped fifteen pounds—although I probably needed to shed those pounds. Justin, on the other hand, lost twenty pounds of every centimeter of fat. His shirt hangs shapeless on his skinny torso. His pants fall down when he sneezes. Weight loss is one of the common risks associated with Crohn's disease, so his damaged digestive track was already crippling his nourishment. Both our reserves were running low, but the fact of the matter is Justin's diaphragm is visible and his body is suffering more than mine.

Of course the boys are game to push into town. We were planning a near-zero day in Wanaka the next day, so why not make it a full zero?

"I wonder what time *Wild* is playing at Cinema Paradiso tomorrow?" I say out loud. The boys don't care as much, but I've been wanting to see *Wild* and it's almost out of the theaters. Plus, I had been hearing about Wanaka's Cinema Paradiso—a place that combines eating and movie watching on comfy sofas—for months. The cinema releases the weekly movie times on Wednesdays, which is today, so I can finally check the schedule.

"Oh my God!" My heart drops. "*Wild* is not playing at the theater tomorrow! Only today!"

"Well what time?" Justin asks as he takes his last bite of streaky bacon.

"5:30." I am about to enter my own personal raincloud.

"Oh come on," Justin comforts. "It's only fifteen miles. We can hoof it."

I don't particularly like having an agenda when hiking, but it is mostly road walking, the weather is fine and a cozy movie night is the prize.

We arrive at the hostel at 4:15 P.M., with enough time to take a shower—for the benefit of the other movie goers—and get to the theater, order our food and sit down for the opening credits. At intermission, Justin and I enjoy our barbecue pizza, homemade salted caramel ice cream and a fresh-baked chocolate chip cookie. The fantasy lives up to its glory.

We wake up late on March 12 with no miles planned, our very first zero day in thirty-five days since starting the South Island.

Wanaka Backpackers has a stellar view of the lake, so we mostly sit on our butts all day eating, starting with a hearty breakfast of streaky bacon, egg and toast. It feels very strange to sit still after being on the constant go for so long, but we wouldn't want to burn too many of those precious calories we loaded at the theater. The hostel Internet allowance is 250 GB, so we can't even make any FaceTime calls to family. We roamed the streets of Wanaka a bit in the search of better and free Internet, but mainly just enjoyed the beautiful day as tourists instead of walkers.

I message back and forth with Matteo, who is about to enter the Richmond Range. He had gotten off trail for a few weeks to work and make some money.

I also read an update from Marilyne, who had gotten stuck with her new hiking group at Goat Pass Hut for three nights because of a rainstorm prohibiting them from criss-crossing the Mingha River and getting into Arthur's Pass. She even ran out of food! I send her a text with my sympathy and a wish for safe river crossing going forward.

Neither Marilyne nor Matteo are planning to come to Queenstown for the hiker party. Given the fact Marilyne is 250 miles behind us, and Matteo nearly five hundred miles behind, I'm pretty certain now that we won't see them again before we leave New Zealand.

Since their completion of the South Island about a month ago, our Appalachian Trail friends, Fern Toe and Thor, have been house sitting nearby to Wanaka. Every week, they e-mailed us detailed South Island information, like that Boyle Village was not a village at all.

We plan to go to an Indian food restaurant with Fern and Thor and invite Kevin.

"So, were Fern Toe's parents hippies?" Kevin asks. "And I'm guessing Thor is Scandinavian?"

"I don't know, why?" I answer.

"With their names, I just figured," Kevin explains.

"Oh geez! Fern Toe and Thor are their trail names!" We all explode in helpless guffaws of laughter.

Our walk out of Wanaka takes us on a gravel path along the lake lined by tall willow and poplar trees shielding the winds. Justin snacks on the last of the homemade cookies Fern Toe baked us as we are strolling along.

One willow stands apart from the rest. It sits in the lake backdropped by the Southern Alps and has quite a distinctive curve to its frame. The tree had humble beginnings seventy years ago as a fence post to keep livestock from grazing, but now is one of New Zealand's most photographed pieces of nature.

On the lake path, we run into a Kiwi, Doug. The seventy-year-old man is section hiking Te Araroa and documenting all 2014-15 southbound and northbound thru hikers he meets by taking pictures and using the hut books. Much like the Kiwi couple we met near Lake Coleridge, Doug's estimate is that 160 people are walking south and forty walking north. That number is a far cry from the thirty total thru hikers on trail in 2011 when it officially opened.

At the end of the lake, we enter the Motatapu Alpine Track. This is another section whose notoriety precedes itself, especially with ten thousand feet of climbing and ten thousand feet of descending in about thirty miles. We were also told to count on some major sidling in those miles. Even after 107 days on Te Araroa, Kiwi's beloved tramping term of sidling still instantly builds sweat in my armpits.

On the other hand, the track supposedly has some of the best huts on the entire trail, thanks to Shania Twain.

Shania Twain, whose real name is Eilleen Lange, and her music producer husband purchased land in New Zealand in 2004 and at the same time, the Te Araroa Trust and Department of Conservation were trying to negotiate land access for Te Araroa through private property. Since Shania was a Canadian making the purchase, the agencies struck a special deal with her. They would allow her to buy the land if she would allow hikers to walk across her hills away from her home and fund the construction of huts and track marking.

Everything—the huts and the hills—lives up to the reputation.

At our second spacious and mouse-free shelter, Roses Hut, another Te Araroa hiker had written:

AFTER TODAY'S HIKE, I FEEL LIKE THE MANLIEST MAN TO HAVE EVER MANNED IT UP IN THE HISTORY OF MEN AND SINCE THE EXISTENCE OF MAN.

I don't disagree with him after gaining six thousand feet and losing six thousand feet of total elevation today, but I respond with a little Shania in my heart:

TYLER, WHAT YOU SHOULD HAVE SAID WAS, 'MAN, I FEEL LIKE A WOMAN!'

We finish up the Motatapu section with a couple from France, Chelsey and Gael. We have the choice to take the high-water route undulating in the bush, or just follow the river. Justin and I have officially turned Kiwi because we embrace the river route with the others.

And since we are corralled into a narrow valley cut by the river, we set a new record and cross the Arrow River sixty-nine times. Submerged in the deep shadows of the mountains, my first steps into the river feel like fifteen cats and dogs biting my toes. As the frost evaporates, lifting the fog from the ground and sunlight hits us, I feel grateful for the refreshing blast.

Prospectors first discovered gold in the Arrow River in the 1800s. Some say there are still treasures to be found, so we keep our heads down searching within the crystal-clear waters, but to no avail.

Road walking means we are nearing Queenstown and passing more and more suburbia, so camping becomes a challenge. Fern Toe promised us there is an established campsite with water and a toilet as soon as we reach the Kawarau River. We see the two-mile section along the river on the map, but no indication of a campsite and it looks like there are houses a stone's throw away.

We breathe a sigh of relief when the neighborhood dissolves into a grove of pine trees along a footpath. We find the secret campsite no problem.

"Beyond this point, this track becomes a veritable trip through Queenstown's dirty laundry basket," I read the trail notes to the boys over two cold instant oat packets for breakfast. "What in the heck does that mean?" It is spitting rain and a little on the chilly side, enough for us to keep our rain shells on.

After passing Queenstown's relegations—the airport, the dog pound, the gun club, the transfer station—I guess I understand the trail notes. But why do the track notes always sound so ominous?

It continues to be a long slog into Queenstown and the marginal weather dampens my mood.

The homestretch comes as we follow an urban pathway along New Zealand's third largest lake, Lake Wakatipu. The craggy mountain range of the Remarkables swirls in the fog, looking like a line of shark's teeth protruding from the opposite side of the lakeshore.

8K TO QUEENSTOWN

I love signs, but we are ticking off the miles at a tortoise pace it seems.

7K TO QUEENSTOWN

My frustration grows as I still see no indication of civilization along the lake's shores and wonder if the distances on the signs are off.

3K TO QUEENSTOWN

We come upon Queenstown Park and Gardens, which has a disc golf course. The tangy scent of the ponderosa pines hits me before I see them and am reminded of home.

"Do you think I can duck behind one of these trees to pee?"

"We're in a really public place. You can't hold it?" Justin quips. "We're almost to Queenstown."

"I've been holding it for miles." I test my visibility behind a tree, but Justin gives me the thumbs down.

The Queenstown Ice Arena comes into view. I waste a few more precious pee-holding minutes looking for a public bathroom around the building. No luck.

Almost immediately, we turn a corner into an alcove

on the lake and there is Queenstown in all its glory. I sprint the last half mile to the public restroom.

With a population of more than thirty thousand and the fact that it is New Zealand's most popular tourist destination, being in Queenstown feels like we've been transplanted into a world with Black Friday crowds.

Along with Chelsey and Gael, we duck into a cafe and order coffees and hot chocolates to warm up. We all agree it's time for lunch in the form of Fergburger.

On our second day in Auckland, someone told us, "You must go to Fergburger in Queenstown." I scribbled it down, but thought nothing of it. Then we heard about it from someone else. And someone else. And other hikers blogged about it. A 2015 CNN article named it "best burger joint on the planet." Fergburger in Queenstown was not to be missed.

Justin opts for the "Mr. Big Stuff," complete with streaky bacon, barbeque sauce and aioli, while I go for "Southern Swine" topped with streaky bacon, avocado, aioli and tomato relish. We add onion rings and the five of us call in our order.

Twenty minutes later, our meals are in hand.

Justin and I part ways with the others to check into our booking at Adventure Queenstown Hostel. Knowing Queenstown was mobbed with tourists, we made a reservation, while the others chose not to. Justin did his research on TripAdvisor and found Adventure Queenstown the top rated, so we were excited to be spending not just one night, but two.

Newly opened in 2011, Adventure Queenstown prides itself in covering all the needs of travellers without nickeling and diming for services. Having been a backpacker across fifty-plus countries himself for many years, hostel owner Brett pays attention to the little details. It's hard not to notice the individual dimmable reading lights and hooks for personal belongings on each bunk, an arsenal of spices, tea and coffee in the community kitchen and towels/hairdryers for use by all guests. One of the best features for us, though, is unlimited WiFi.

We spend the rest of the rainy day not leaving the hostel except to resupply. We eat a half gallon of Tip Top Boysenberry Ripple Ice Cream in spurts, FaceTime all our family and do things on the Internet we couldn't normally do. I catch up on all the Te Araroa hiker blogs. What else? I have no idea what is going on in the world right now. News of war? Videos of kittens being funny? One of the Kardashians getting divorced? None of that I care for, but if I wanted to, I have the time and bandwidth to check.

Monday nights at Adventure Queenstown Hostel are movie nights, meaning they pick a new release to show in the hostel's massive lounge and make popcorn to share among the guests. We watch the back-to-back movies: *The Imitation Game*, the historical drama about mathematician Alan Turing during World War II, and *What We Do In The Shadows*. Much more lighthearted, *What We Do In The Shadows* is a New Zealand mockumentary horror comedy film about vampires living in Wellington. We had no idea what to expect, yet we could not take our eyes away; that's how oddly hilarious the film was.

On Tuesday, we head out for the long-awaited Hiker Trash Party at 2 P.M. at Pog Mahones Irish Bar, where the Irish couple have reserved a private space for us. Alan and Lauren greet us immediately. They had just finished their trek in Bluff on March 15th and raced up to Queenstown to host the party and celebrate. Their elation was palpable, and it was then I realized we, ourselves, had only two hundred miles of the trail yet, probably less than two weeks of walking.

No time for nostalgia or deep thoughts; more familiar faces trickled in—Serina, David, Carolyn and Dan, then a few we hadn't seen since the North Island—Jeremiah, Kelsey and Florian. We chitchat about where we are on the trail and slam the South Island's biggest hassles, like tussock and the river crossings.

Many of our other comrades behind us—Matteo, Marilyne, Eef, PJ and Patrick—as well as those names I've come to know in the hut books or on blogs, could not make it. Ole chose to forge ahead, hopping in front of us once again and plans to complete the trail within a week. Serina tells us Nicolas quit the trail. The grand total at the gathering is twenty-five, which is still impressive. Justin and I stay for the group picture at 5 P.M., but we both have a one-drink tolerance at this point—who am I kidding, I've always had a one-drink tolerance—and decide an increasingly loud bar was not our thing.

We treat ourselves to a second Fergburger takeaway and polish off the rest of our ice cream at our hostel.

The next section presents another natural break in the trail because of Lake Wakatipu. While Te Araroa Trust is planning to add a route from Queenstown to Glenorchy in the future, right now it is up to us on how we want to reach the Greenstone Track trailhead on the complete opposite shore of the lake.

Some people are hiring a charter boat the twenty-five miles across the lake. Two American brothers who we've yet to meet are walking the fifty road miles to the other side. They are adamant about walking every mile—they never hitchhike to towns for resupply and are the only two who attempted, unsuccessfully, to cross the Rakaia River.

We had called the water taxi company, who quoted us $600 for the ride to the trailhead. A $52 per person road shuttle around the lake for the next morning at 8 A.M. sounded much more appealing.

The misty mountains surrounding Lake Wakatipu on the Glenorchy side serve as the scene used in *The Lord of the Rings* ads. The drive around takes us about three hours, so I can't imagine what it took the brothers to walk.

On trail, we follow a Grade A track to the popular Greenstone Hut, part of the Caples and Greenstone tracks. Both can be linked with one of the Great Walks, the Routeburn Track, hence their fame.

We veer off from the Greenstone Hut and the track deteriorates to bogs and tussock on steroids. We tread lightly when we see two young guys sleeping off the trail.

"I think those were the brothers from Atlanta," I whisper to Justin and Kevin once we find distance from them. "I guess the extra walking did them in."

At Taipo Hut, the three of us cozy in for the night as the wind howls the symphony of "don't go outside" all night long. My watch reads thirty-four degrees at 7:45 A.M., and Justin and I heat our instant oats in an effort to keep our blood flowing.

About one mile from the hut, on a fairly simple rock hop across a river, Kevin eats it, full body. He pops up, soaking wet. I stand paralyzed, trying to find the right words or actions. Rightfully pissed—but in his usual good spirits nonetheless—he tells us he will catch up after changing his clothing and shoes.

Nearly twenty miles later, the three of us set up camp in the forest along the Maroroa River. Kevin's clothes and shoes are still not completely dry from the morning dip, but nothing dampens his mood. As we are all eating our respective dinners on downed logs, two tousled, skinny men pass. They are moving at a clip and if I didn't yell out to them, they probably would have just passed.

"Are you the brothers from Atlanta?" I blurt.

"We are," one informs. They stop, but I can tell they really want to keep moving. I tick through the questions in my head.

"Did you really cross the Rakaia? And have you really avoided hitchhiking completely? Even for towns like Arthur's Pass or Methven?"

"We tried to cross the Rakaia, but only made it halfway before being stranded on a rocky bed with rising waters. We camped, but eventually turned back," one brother admits. I can see a combination of exhaustion and hunger etched into his face.

"And, yes, we've walked every mile possible from Cape Reinga."

I marvel at their dedication to purity, and while I still have more questions, I let them go. Clearly, they have miles on their minds.

Minutes later, a couple decked out in knee-high gaiters and large backpacks going northbound saunters to a stop at our camp.

"How's the Department of Conservation campground north of here?"

"It's fine, nothing special," Kevin answers. "But there are plenty of spots to freedom camp along the lake."

"Okay, thanks." The male does all the talking. I am trying to make out his accent, but am not sure there is one. He looks to be in his late forties, while she looks in her twenties. "She's going to be the first Thai woman to walk Te Araroa," he says proudly. "We know we will hit winter, but she is tough." She stands quietly and looks miserable. He adds, "you have tough terrain coming up. There's some mud ahead. And beach walking. It took us twenty-five days to get here."

"Twenty-five days?" Justin's shock is undeniable. We estimate about ten days to Bluff.

We find a way to wrap up this uncomfortable conversation—thinking how often we are given information we really could have done without—and send the odd twosome on their way,

Once they are out of sight, I ask seriously, "Do you think she has been kidnapped?"

| 15 |

The Homestretch
Days 114-123: 171.8 miles

Our last nine days on the trail are tough. With fall coming and every step bringing us closer to the forty-fifth parallel—the midway point between the South Pole and the Equator—our walking routine presents us with fewer precious minutes of daylight. We hardly move in our tent before 7:15 A.M., naturally matching the sun's rhythm with the changing season. Windswept by the arctic gales of the Southern Ocean, the unprotected coast creates a funnel of air that stiffens our joints. Every day, it rains just a little.

The landscape also changes for a few days. Bony mountain ranges surrender to softer and highly productive farming hills thanks to the rain shadow affecting Southland and the Fiordland. Sheep abound among commercial deer lots and dairy farms. We are pretty certain out of the thirty-one million sheep across New Zealand, we've seen at least ten thousand by this point. Or at least stepped in sheep feces ten thousand times.

Among all the agriculture, we struggle to find a campsite one night. We knock on a few doors to inquire about permission to camp, but no one is home. Our choice is to illegally camp or risk being run over by farm equipment while sleeping on the narrow gravel roads.

We walk up a hill to a fence line of one seemingly vacant property, well out of view of the road. I pull out Jamaican Rice and Chicken to make for dinner. Kevin sits down with his own dinner concoction against the fence, but jumps back up immediately.

"I think I just got shocked by the fence." He says as he rubs his back.

I furrow my brow and assure, "It doesn't look at all electric. Are you sure?"

"I mean, I felt something," Kevin chuckles.

"I dare you to test it babe," Justin provokes. "Go for it."

Arrogantly, I reach out and the world momentarily recedes into pale colors as I feel a jolt through my arm.

"Retribution for camping illegally?" Kevin smirks. The rest of the night, thankfully goes smoother.

Thanks to a hospitable postal worker who already has David in his truck the next morning, we cram in among the packages to hitch a ride to Te Anau for a quick resupply. Kevin is a trooper and rides in the back flatbed for the eighteen-mile trip. Te Anau, the gateway to Fiordland National Park and Milford Sound, a world heritage area, is swarming with tourists. David stays for a night, but we merely make it a three-hour detour.

Back on the trail under stormy skies, we enter the moss-encrusted, ancient-looking beech forest of the forty-mile Takitimu Range. Justin and I are immediately reminded of the hardships we experienced four months earlier in the woodlands of Herekino and Rataea. In the miserable beauty of the forest, the whole path looks like a piece of Earth completely turned over. The mud penetrates every thread of clothing, even with our rain gear on.

"Seriously, the mud was worse than this?" Kevin laments.

He thrashes ahead on the claustrophobic trail in frustration, but Justin and I lag about as fast as a funeral procession. We see Kevin leaving Aparima Hut as we are walking down to it. A sign for Lower Wairaki Hut reads sixteen kilometers, while our notes claim thirteen.

"Ugh, I can barely do thirteen more kilometers, let alone sixteen," I cry.

"Let's just camp," Justin pitches. "These huts are not the most appealing anyway."

Two hours later, we struggle to find a flat or dry-ish spot, but instead settle on the only option versus right on the trail: a spongy mattress of ferns and moss. The night was weirdly silent.

When we pop out of the forest two days later, the three of us decide a side trip to Otautau for a warm shower would be just the boost we need to finish strongly. Fern Toe had told us about Otautau's campground that offers a camp spot, shower and laundry for $10—a tidbit not included in our trail notes. Surrounded by private lands, our camping options are limited, so it's sensible.

Kevin decides after twenty minutes of three cars passing us by, he would walk the six miles into town.

"One more car," I promise Justin while trying to shake more mud off my rain pants.

Ten minutes later, Shane picks us up in a truck and when we don't see Kevin walking on the road, we realize he also scored a ride.

With laundry in motion, the three of us dodge raindrops to the Otautau Hotel and Pub for dinner. I order a salad and the half portion of the "Absolutely Apricot" pizza—complete with an apricot base, chicken, cheese and apricot swirl—while Justin orders the blue cod platter. Before we came to New Zealand, someone advised us not to expect too much about the food, but we truly believe we've tried some of the more unique and delicious dishes ever. And it has not just been the hiker hunger talking.

Light rain continues in the morning as we make our way along columns of eucalyptus trees, peaking my olfactory senses. Eventually, we enter the thirty-three-mile, wet and wild Longwood Forest Track.

The octaves of the orange markers are brighter than a prison jumpsuit, standing out amongst the dystopian landscape where shadows turn into people and back into shadows within a blink of the eye. We duck wrist-thick branches of rimu and totara trees, a myriad of spider highways crisscrossing the path like fishing nets, not to mention foliage dangling like tinsel. Crawling through the cave of impalement tools tugging on our backpacks, we thrust through the tangled forest for the last time on our entire trek.

Above the treeline, isolated storm clouds sail the sky dragging anchors of rain. Now and then, one passes over us, unloading its spatter. It is cold enough to crack a stone. Club moss covers the trail and groundwater fills our boots, turning our feet into cement blocks of ice. Even with gloves on, the dampness in the air worries me that my hands may freeze to my trekking poles.

"Have you s-s-s-seen a m-m-marker?" I chatter, turning myself in a full circle to scan the entire marshland as wind-provoked tears cling to the creases in my eyes. There are supposed to be views of our endpoint, Bluff, from up here, but I see nothing but the inside of a ping-pong ball.

We turn our back to the wind and rain and pull out the iPhone. I stab my numb, shriveled fingers at the screen, pulling up the iHikeGPS NZ app.

"This way," I point south.

On the other side of the hill, we reenter Longwood, catching up to Kevin for lunch, finding the most sheltered spot in the rain.

An owl—potentially a morepork, New Zealand's only native owl—lands on a nearby branch.

"I would be concerned, but it's so dark in this forest, I bet the owl thinks it's night," I jest.

Two new-to-us Te Araroa hikers have splayed their belongings around the four-person Martin's Hut, built in 1905. Justin and I retreat to our tent, which feels like a palace compared with the musty hut. I steal the Intentions Book to make my last entry. Flipping through the pages, so many names—Marilyne, Matteo, Jeremiah, Kelsey, Florian, Rod, Eef, PJ, Patrick, Rob, Joss, Serina, Nicolas, David—have disappeared now that they are behind us. Andrew, another hiker we had not met, but had been seeing in print for months, had to bail on his hike a mere one hundred miles from Bluff because of a broken ankle in the Takitimu Forest. He plans to return and finish months later.

I have no energy to write anything profound on the one line provided, so I simply add on March 25, 2015:

BLUFF FOUND! 123 DAYS IN THE MAKING!

The last bit of forest is along a historic watercourse frozen in time from more than a century ago. In the 1890s, the Chinese set up a town nearby and mined for gold in the Longwoods. The leftover sluicing corridor through the forest is a zigzag of steep-banked irrigation ditches. Engulfed in mud, we finally drop back on the road to Colac Bay just in time for the rain to completely stop.

As if Te Araroa continues to come full circle, we face a twenty-mile beach section. Under thick clouds, keeping us cool, we pass the miles with a few more inquiries from the Book of Questions. We have covered roughly one hundred and fifty questions during our fifty days with Kevin.

The beach is as desolate as usual, save for a few cars buried in the sand. The waves are creeping steadily toward us as we approach high tide for one last time.

That night, camped in the dunes, we eat our last Beef Stroganoff—reluctantly because we are still turned off by this meal choice, but also because it feels wrong to be so close to the end. I am oscillating between sad and relieved.

On one hand, pain had taken up residence in my whole body. I don't want to hike another mile. I don't want to eat oatmeal for breakfast every morning. I want my feet to be dry for more than three hours. I want my husband to stop looking like a grasshopper with a massive beard. I want to watch Netflix movies from the comfort of a bed with eight hundred threat count sheets and a blanket. I fantasize about rainy days during our upcoming trip to Sydney and just snuggling up to a good movie. We are a half a world away from home and I also look forward to the comforts of family and friends again.

I am certain I am coming away from the trail reset and

reshaped with an altered perspective on life, just like I did on the Appalachian Trail. Learning to adapt to the brutal nature of Te Araroa helped me shed a few more of my Type A inclinations. I am reminded that there are always going to be bumps in life, but they also present an opportunity to rise above adversity.

As a couple, Te Araroa strengthened our partnership. Even though this Type II fun is where our marriage feels the most alive, and those periods of suffering punctuated by glee and the enormous sense of accomplishment are our kryptonite, it's the moments that almost broke us that actually built us up.

Marriage is a lifetime of learning. It's also sandpaper to the ego. If Justin is the catalyst for audacious dreams, I am the reason they can unfold. We aren't going to change each other; we're going to capitalize on our individual strengths and weaknesses.

We live, work and play together. Our marriage can't be fifty-fifty; it needs to compensate when necessary. On trails, we can't go our separate ways or let issues escalate. We pick our battles and diffuse any tension on the spot. Te Araroa required us to rely on each other so much, and in turn, helped us practice effective communication. And if we want to continue marching to a beat of a different drum in life, we needed this relationship harmony practice.

If we had a dollar for every time a stranger heard our abridged love story and said, "If you can survive long-distance hiking, you can survive anything together," we'd be rich. I wouldn't know it yet, but in exactly nineteen months, I would be sitting by Justin's bedside in a hospital for the first of three Crohn's-related surgeries within a two-year span. Instead of the weight of my backpack and trail logistics, I would be carrying the weight of disease and the unchartered territory of being a young caretaker.

Thoughts about the euphoria of our long-distance hike completion—divided by a fogginess of total bliss and bone-deep tiredness—lull me to sleep.

Our final night of the trek lands us in Invercargill, the most populated city in the Southland. I wish we are tenting, but I am sharing a bunkroom with nine strangers, Kevin and my husband. Less than twenty-two miles on tar sealed roads stand between us and Bluff.

Invercargill is also the town where Mike lives—the Mike who gave us a hitch way up on the North Island early on our hike and told us to give him a shout. Earlier in the week, I posted this message on Te Araroa's 2014-15 Facebook page:

"Anyone know Mike from Invercargill? He gave us a ride in December out of Puhoi and told us to look him up when we got down here... we should be in Invercargill on Saturday the 28th!"

Mike immediately messaged me back. Turns out, though, he is out of town the day we are in Invercargill.

Under perfect conditions on March 29, 2015, we make our way to the southern extremity of New Zealand, the blustery port town of Bluff. My heart and stomach trade places as the last four miles take us through the hills looking out to the Foveaux Strait.

Kevin is ahead of us and we are catching up to an older gentleman strolling on the trail. He turns as Kevin passes him and it is Mike from Invercargill. He is holding a bottle of champagne in his hand.

"I felt so awful I wasn't around yisterday, I decided to

try to catch you at the signpost!"

Full circle, Te Araroa, full circle.

As we turn the corner, a yellow signpost bristles with a bunch of distances of the world as the crow flies, but there is only one place that stands out.

CAPE REINGA 1401 KILOMETERS

This trail may have been the most masochistic route to explore New Zealand with a beating that won't soon be forgotten, but we chose the atypical path once again. The human-powered route allowed us to truly experience the great diversity of the country—the wild coastline, the alpine forests (jungles), the rolling farmland, the active and dormant volcanoes, the towering mountain passes, the crystal clear lakes, the sweeping river valleys, the rural settlements, the big cities and most importantly, the incomprehensible hospitality and generosity of the people. The trail had us tapping nearly every skill we'd learned in previous adventures and after all is said and done, I am happy to call it vacation-slideshow perfect. We may have been walking in search of the highs, but the lows made for some of the best stories.

Who can say they have walked the entire length of a country? Who can say they spent 123 days walking more than two thousand miles? Who can say they spent seventy-one nights out of 122 nights in a tent? Who can say they only took thirty-five showers during the past four months?

We can.

The achievement of Te Araroa is a trophy on our shelf. And because of the trail, we are more equipped—individually and as a couple—for what's next.

| Te Araroa Gear List |

Backpacks
Justin - Gregory Baltoro 65 (2015 version)
Weight: 4lbs 12 oz
Patrice - Gregory Deva 60 (2015 version)
Weight: 4lbs 6oz

Tent
Big Agnes Copper Spur UL2 Tent (updated 2014)
Weight: 3 lbs 2 oz

Sleep System
Justin
Therm-a-Rest Auriga 35 degree down blanket (750+
    fill goose down with an elasticized footbox)
Weight: 1lb, 5 oz
Cocoon Silk Mummy Liner
Weight: 4.7 oz
Therm-a-Rest XLite Pad (2013 version) (R-Value 3.2)
Weight: 12 oz
Universal sheet
Weight: 3.7 oz
Nemo Fillo Pillow (J's comfort item)
Weight: 10.8 oz
Patrice

Therm-a-Rest Antares HD 20-degree bag
Weight: 2 lbs
Coolmax Cocoon Mummy Liner
Weight: 9 oz
Therm-a-Rest XLite Pad (2015 version) (R-Value 3.2, longer length 6")
Weight: 12 oz

Footwear
Justin
Hi-Tec Altitude Trek Low Waterproof
Hi-Tec Rio Adventure (for recovery and river crossings)
Weight: 8 oz
Superfeet Carbon Insoles (2 different pairs)
Patrice
Hi-Tec Ohio Waterproof (with moisture-wicking lining)
Weight: 13.8 oz
Hi-Tec Zuuks (for recovery and river crossings)
Weight: 4.8 oz
Superfeet Berry and Carbon Insoles (switched out halfway)

Water Filter
Sawyer Mini Water Filter (64 oz and 16 oz bags)
Weight: 2 oz for filter and 6.5 oz for bags
Sawyer Inline Filter on our hydration bladders
Weight: 1.8 oz

Cookware
MSR PocketRocket

Weight: 3 oz
GSI Outdoors Halulite MicroDualist
Weight: 18 oz
2 GSI Outdoors Titanium Kung Foon
Weight: 4.1 oz (each)

Patrice's Clothing
Sea to Summit Dry Bag/Stuff Sack
2 pairs of ExOfficio Give and Go Undies
2 Sports Bras
Merrell wicking tee
REI wicking tee
REI wicking long-sleeved tee
REI Sahara Pants (convertible to capris)
REI yoga-type pants for sleeping/town
LL Bean long johns
Ex Officio Rain Logic Jacket
Marmot Rain pants
Big Agnes 700 fill DownTek Shovelhead Jacket (15 oz)
2 pairs of hiking socks
1 pair of sleeping socks

Justin's Clothing
Therm-a-rest Dry Bag/Stuff Sack
2 pairs of ExOfficio Give and Go Boxers
Salomon wicking tee
Patagonia base layer tee
ExOfficio SoCool long sleeve 1/2 zip
Mountain Hardwear Covertible Pack Pants
Patagonia long underwear
Marmot Rain Pants
Marmot Crux Raincoat

Big Agnes 700 fill DownTek Shovelhead Jacket (15oz)
2 pairs of hiking socks
1 pair of sleeping socks

Headlights
Princeton Tec Vizz (1 for each person - 3.2 oz)

Trekking Poles
Patrice
Helinox Passport Tension Lock Adjustable Poles
Weight: 10 oz
Justin
Helinox Passport Tension Lock Poles
Weight: 12 oz

Misc
GSI Outdoors Cathole Trowel
Weight: 3.1 oz
Granite Gear 18L Ultrasil Stuff Sack (food bag)
Weight: 21 grams
PowerTraveller Solar Monkey Adventurer Solar Charger
Weight: 9.3 oz
Garmin Fenix Watch
Weight: 3.1 oz
SPOT Satellite Messenger – Gen 2
Weight: 4 oz
Passport/License
2 Headnets
iPhone 5c and charger
iPad Mini
Sawyer First Aid Kit

| Acknowledgements |

There are so many people who've encouraged me as a writer and/or contributed to this book in some shape or form. A handful of the people, I've known for a lifetime. Others were a quick meeting. But I wholeheartedly believe that my journey as a writer and the ability to tell my stories wouldn't be possible without the following folks.

From the bottom of my heart, thank you to ...

*My husband. Justin. You are my biggest cheerleader, my audacious dreamer and the catalyst to our adventures. We may calculate risks and tackle to-do lists differently, but I couldn't ask for a better partner in life and love. Your unwavering support and encouragement for my writing pursuits and this book are much appreciated, as is your ability to send me into laughing hysterias.

*My family. Dad, you'd be so proud. You were always the #1 fan of my writing and set the example to be a voracious reader. I wish you could be alive to see my book in print. Mom, you're the very best listener, even though I know you can't quite grasp the subject matter of hiking and publishing, your undivided attention and boundless enthusiasm was just what I needed time and time again.

And my sister, Janice, your ability to persevere through hardships with a genuine smile on your face has taught me more than you'll ever know.

*Trail Angels. New Zealand's hospitality is inherent to their culture, so while none of the strangers we met thought they were doing anything more than just living normally, let me remind you all how impactful your generosity was for us. The list is too long, but I especially want to give gigantic gratitude to Carole & Tony and Max & Lyn, who took us in for days.

*Trail Framily. I'd be remiss if I didn't express my respect and gratitude to all the other long-distance hikers out there, not just on Te Araroa, but all trails. There's something about backpacking that bonds you immediately—probably that shared willingness to pull on wet socks in your cramped tent so you can make the miles when outside temps are barely above freezing. Cheers to Kevin, Marilyne and Matteo, who hiked alongside us for many miles on Te Araroa and know more about our experience in New Zealand than anyone. And an ode to Second Nature, So Gr8ful, Fire Marshall, Sniffles, Shadow, Country Mouse, Fern Toe and Bolt, our original trail community. We have met some lifelong friends in the wild. And crossing paths with y'all—whether it's on the trail or on the road—only solidifies our strong connection.

*Te Araroa Trust. No one really needs a reason to visit New Zealand, but building a continuous pathway gave us all another excuse, and challenge. Geoff Chapple had a dream of a national trail, and turned it into a reality. The

Te Araroa Trust has done a fantastic job building the trail up, spreading awareness and preserving the wild so people like Justin and I can take a hike. Keep up the good work!

*My writer friends. The act of writing is solitary—and sometimes lonesome—work. When you have others who get it, that makes all the difference. First and foremost, thank you to Leanne (who also happens to be my mother-in-law), Mary, Heather, Misti, Jenn, Donna, Liz and all the friends from my Patchwork Farms Writing Retreat. You all played a huge role in this specific project, whether it was a dose of inspiration, encouragement, editing or insight. This book would be vastly different if I hadn't been able to talk "shop" to gain your tried and true guidance and advice. Beyond the book, there's been so many others in my life who boosted my writing career. Thank you, Lynn, who gave me my first newspaper assignment when I was in the 7th grade. Thank you Christine, Sue, Jen, Jared, Lynne, Shannon and Brian, who shared endless hours in the King's College newspaper office eating greasy food from Rodano's, while putting out a quality product every other week. Thank you to Backpacker Magazine for giving me my start in outdoor writing.

*The various gear companies who have supported our endeavors over the years. We quickly learned which products were our favs during our first thru hike in 2011, and though we continue to test newer gear and cull out other brands for writing projects, we have some go-to favorites. Specifically, thanks to Gregory, Therm-a-Rest, Sawyer, Superfeet, Big Agnes, Backpackers Pantry,

CloudLine, SPOT and Powertraveller. Not only did you outfit us with the actual gear to succeed on Te Araroa, but you've supported many of our crazy ideas over the years and our 2017 New Zealand Speaking Tour.

*My blog readers. I started our "Life Less Ordinary" blog in 2008 as a way to connect with friends around the country and share pictures. The audience has grown more than I ever could have hoped, and I extend my heartfelt appreciation to dedicated readers.
www.wanderinglavignes.com

*Leave No Trace Center for Outdoor Ethics. We are so glad we finally got a chance to work for the nonprofit and be a part of the core team, after years of being sideline "super fans."

*Atmosphere Press. Thanks to everyone who helped me produce the best version of my work, especially Nick and Kyle!

| About Atmosphere Press |

Atmosphere Press is an independent, full-service publisher for excellent books in all genres and for all audiences. Learn more about what we do at atmospherepress.com.

We encourage you to check out some of Atmosphere's latest releases, which are available at Amazon.com and via order from your local bookstore:

Geometry of Fire, nonfiction by Paul Warmbier

Chasing the Dragon's Tail, nonfiction by Craig Fullerton

Pandemic Aftermath: How Coronavirus Changed Global Society, nonfiction by Trond Undheim

Great Spirit of Yosemite: The Story of Chief Tenaya, nonfiction by Paul Edmondson

My Cemetery Friends: A Garden of Encounters at Mount Saint Mary in Queens, New York, nonfiction and poetry by Vincent J. Tomeo

Change in 4D, nonfiction by Wendy Wickham

Disruption Games: How to Thrive on Serial Failure, nonfiction by Trond Undheim

| About the Author |

Patrice La Vigne is a freelance writer whose work has been featured in *Backpacker, Outside, REI Co-Op Journal, Gear-Junkie* and *SNEWS*. Although she and her husband, Justin, are self-proclaimed nomads who spend most of their time working on the road, their home base is a dry cabin outside of Denali  National Park and Preserve in Alaska. Patrice has hiked more than 6,000 miles, including the Appalachian Trail, and is close to her goal of visiting all the National Parks and climbing the state high points.

To follow Patrice's adventures, read her articles and see pictures of her and Justin's Te Araroa thru hike, visit www.wanderinglavignes.com.

CPSIA information can be obtained
at www.ICGtesting.com
Printed in the USA
FSHW010803111020
74632FS